# DOUBLE WEAVE

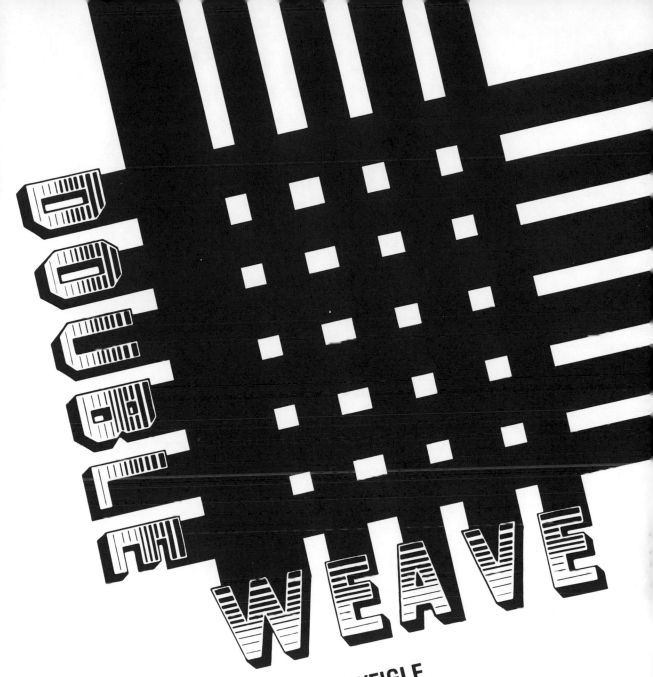

# DOUBLE WEAVE

## BY PALMY WEIGLE

WATSON-GUPTILL PUBLICATIONS/NEW YORK
PITMAN PUBLISHING/LONDON

*To Klara Cherepov*

Copyright © 1978 by Watson-Guptill Publications

First published 1978 in the United States and Canada by Watson-Guptill Publications,
a division of Billboard Publications, Inc.
1515 Broadway, New York, New York 10036

**Library of Congress Cataloging in Publication Data**
Weigle, Palmy, 1920–
  Double weave.
  Bibliography: p.
  Includes index.
  1. Hand weaving.  I. Title
TT848.W378    746.1′4    78–9653
ISBN 0–8230–1355–3

Published in Great Britain by Pitman Publishing
39 Parker Street, London WC2B  5PB
ISBN 0-273-01286-X

Manufactured in U.S.A.

First Printing, 1978
Second Printing, 1980

# Contents

# Acknowledgments

My thanks to friends, students, and fellow weavers who contributed so much to the making of this book: To Libby Crawford of Michigan for initially arousing my interest in the many facets of double weave. To Marjory Payne and others who encouraged my teaching of double-weave techniques. To Judy Spark, Eileen Caruso, and Laurene Ouellette for designing and weaving projects for the book. To Sr. Mary Jane Robertshaw for her encouragement and constant understanding. To Osma Gallinger Tod for her generosity in making available the designs for *The Weaver's Creed* and *The Lord is My Shepherd.* To Ruth Geneslaw, Malina Kern, Jean Farley, Eva Quinn, Dolly Curtis, Lynn Fischer, Mary Studeny, Chris Daley, Peggy Manja, Meg Little, and Greta Klingenburg who kindly furnished photographs of their weavings. To Lewis Knauss for his help and advice. To Carole Shortt for doing such a fine job in photographing many of the pictures for the book. To Jennifer Place who has guided me through not only this book but also the previous two. Last but by no means least, my thanks for so many things to Klara Cherepov, whose talents as a teacher and weaver are matched only by her warmth and kindness as a friend.

# Introduction

Double weave as a textile technique has been found in many cultures throughout the world. The ancient Peruvians, using primitive looms, understood very well how to produce double cloth for garments and straps, tubular weave for bags, and pick-up work for symbolic designs. Chinese civilizations, centuries before the birth of Christ, are known to have woven delicate double and even triple cloth.

In modern times, the use of double weave has been extensive throughout the European countries, from Spain and Italy in the south to the Scandinavian countries and Great Britain in the north. In Finland, the decorative pick-up work became highly developed in a method known today as *Finnweave.* More practical applications of double weave included weaving tubular fabrics for fire hose and pipe coverings. Today, in the handcraft shops in Spain, handbags and capes woven in reversible double weave are favorite items of trade offered to the tourist.

In the western hemisphere, Indian tribes of northwestern Mexico, working with backstrap looms, made double cloth with intricate designs. Fine examples can also be found in weavings from Guatemala and Bolivia as well as from Peru and Ecuador.

During the colonial period in America, the most popular pieces produced in double weave were coverlets with elaborate patterns and fancy names like Whig Rose and Snowball. The coverlets were usually woven in white and indigo blue, but occasionally the yarn was dyed red with madder. The beautiful double-weave coverlets of eastern Canada in the nineteenth century were likewise primarily of indigo-dyed wool and white cotton, with brown or yellow wool and linen sometimes used instead of cotton.

In art fabrics of today, double weave is of great importance. Wall hangings with imaginative designs in the pick-up technique can be found in most fiber exhibitions. Woven tubes are shaped to form fiber sculptures; layers are interchanged and stuffed with fleece, multiple wefts, and preshaped foam rubber. Double weave is also called on to create flaps and pleats to give three-dimensional quality to a woven piece.

It must be understood that not all fabrics labeled double weave can be produced with a four-harness loom; for example, some of the elaborate patterns of the coverlets require 16 or more harnesses. However, weavers who have just four harnesses on their looms should not be discouraged; there are a great many possibilities of double weave open to them. The purpose of this book is to provide instruction in the basic techniques of double weave for the four-harness loom. Detailed directions will also be given for projects that include ponchos, pillows, blankets, and wall hangings.

## WHAT IS DOUBLE WEAVE?

*Double weave* is the ability to produce two layers of cloth simultaneously across the width of the warp on a four-harness loom. To understand the concept, you must bear in mind that two harnesses are needed to make one layer of cloth in the simplest weave, the plain weave.

To produce a plain weave, or *tabby* as it is sometimes called, the warp is threaded on two harnesses with the threads alternating between the two harnesses. Then by raising one harness, half of the warp threads are raised to create a shed through which one shot of weft is passed. Next the other harness is raised to bring up the other half of the warp threads making a shed for the second weft shot. This procedure of raising the two harnesses alternately and weaving a weft shot each time produces one layer of fabric in plain weave.

If two harnesses can produce one layer of fabric, then a four-harness loom can produce two layers of fabric, two harnesses for each layer. By manipulating the harnesses properly, those two layers may be entirely separate from each other, they may be joined at either the right-hand or the left-hand side, or at both sides to form a tube. One layer may be a lace weave while the other is a plain weave. The two layers may be stitched together at intervals; they may be quilted and stuffed. The two layers may exchange positions, with the top layer becoming the bottom layer and vice versa. Designs may be picked up from the bottom layer against a background of the top layer. Double weave can even become three-dimensional. The exercises in this book are designed to teach you the many possibilities of double weave on a four-harness loom.

There are two basic ways of threading a loom for double weave. One method places the warp threads for one layer on harnesses 1 and 2, with the warp threads for the other layer on harnesses 3 and 4. The second method places the warp threads for one layer on harnesses 1 and 3, with the warp threads for the other layer on harnesses 2 and 4. The second method is the preferred one, because the warp threads for each layer are more evenly distributed across the width of the warp. If the top layer is threaded on harnesses 1 and 3, by raising alternately harness 1 and harness 3 and weaving one shot each time, the upper layer of fabric can be woven. In order to weave the lower layer of fabric, all the warp threads of the upper layer must be raised out of the way and half of the warp threads must be raised alternately with the other half of the lower warp threads, each time passing a weft shot through the shed created. In other words, to weave the bottom layer, you raise harnesses 1 and 3 (the top layer warp threads) and harness 2 (half the lower warp threads) for one shot; for the second shot, you raise harnesses 1 and 3 and harness 4 (the other half of the lower warp threads). This is the principle on which double weave is based. Once understood, the double weave possibilities of the four-harness loom are open to you.

*Note:* You can find photographs of key projects and exercises, as well as a gallery of finished pieces, on pages 81–96.

# PART ONE:

# DOUBLE LAYERS, TUBULAR WEAVE, AND DOUBLE-WIDTH FABRIC

The exercises in Part One will serve to introduce you to the basic concepts of double weave. In the beginning, you'll become familiar with how the harnesses control the individual layers and how they can be manipulated to allow the top layer to become the bottom layer, and vice versa. You'll produce simple lace weaves on the top layer against a backdrop of a plain weave on the bottom.

Next, you'll join the two layers at both sides to make a tube or a series of tubes across the width of the warp—tubes that may be stuffed or not, and that may be joined together or woven separately side by side. Double weave can also be used to make layers that are joined at only one side, not just for tubes with the top and bottom closed, but also for fabric whose width is twice that produced normally on the loom. Double-width fabric can be a real boon to weavers working on narrow-width looms who want to make clothing. Directions will be given for garments that can be woven even on 20-in (51-cm) looms. At the end of this first series of exercises, suggestions based on the material covered will also be given for other projects.

## MAKING SEPARATE WARPS FOR EACH EXERCISE

For those of you who would like to do each series of exercises on a separate warp, I'll give directions for making a 2 yd (1.8-m) warp. A warp of this length will be enough to do the exercises in Part Two. Parts Three and Four will each require a separate warp, 2 yd (1.8 m) long.

For these exercises, use a yarn of a smooth, strong fiber; No. 5 perle cotton or a thin two-ply worsted yarn would be good choices. Select two colors with a good contrast, such as black and white or beige and dark brown. The strong contrast will be helpful in distinguishing between the two layers in the weaving process. Throughout this book, I'll designate the two colors color A and color B.

In figuring the number of threads needed for the warp, bear in mind that each inch (2.5 cm) of warp will have an equal number of threads of color A and color B. Therefore, the number of threads or ends per inch (or per 2.5 cm)—abbreviated *epi*—will be twice the number needed for one layer of fabric. Thus, for a fabric with 15 ends to the inch, 30 ends are needed: 15 of color A and 15 of color B. The recommended density for either the No. 5 perle cotton or the thin two-ply worsted is 15 or 16 ends to the inch for each layer.

To do the exercises in Part Two, prepare a warp 8 in (20 cm) wide, 2 yd (1.8 m) long.

### For 15 Ends Per Inch in a 15-Dent Reed

Each layer will have 15 ends to the inch (2.5 cm), with 120 ends (15 epi × 8 in or 20 cm) of color A and 120 ends (15 epi × 8 in or 20 cm) of color B, making a total of 240 ends.

120 ends color A × 2 yd (1.8 m) long = 240 yd (218 m) color A warp yarn
120 ends color B × 2 yd (1.8 m) long = 240 yd (218 m) color B warp yarn

For ease in preparing the warp, tie the end of the color A yarn and the end of the color B yarn together and warp two ends at a time.

*Threading the Loom.* Use a straight threading, 1–2–3–4, alternating one end of color A with one end of color B. Color A will be on harnesses 1 and 3, while color B will be on harnesses 2 and 4.

Start threading at the right-hand side of the loom and work from right to left. Harness 1 is the one closest to you at the front, and harness 4 is the last one at the back of the loom. After you've finished threading, to be sure that you've threaded correctly, raise harnesses 1 and 3; only color A warp threads should be raised. Raise harnesses 2 and 4; only color B threads should be raised.

*Sleying the Reed.* Use the center 8 in (20 cm) on a 15-dent reed. The warp will be sleyed two threads per dent, one thread color A and one thread color B all across the 8 in (20 cm) of the warp.

## For 16 Ends Per Inch in an Eight-Dent Reed

Each layer will have 16 ends to the inch (2.5 cm), with 128 ends (16 epi × 8 in or 20 cm) of color A and 128 ends (16 epi × 8 in or 20 cm) of color B, making a total of 256 ends.

128 ends color A × 2 yd (1.8 m) long = 256 yd (233 m) color A warp yarn
128 ends color B × 2 yd (1.8 m) long = 256 yd (233 m) color B warp yarn

For ease in preparing the warp, tie the end of the color A yarn and the end of the color B yarn together and warp two ends at a time.

*Threading the Loom.* Use a straight threading, 1–2–3–4, alternating one end of color A with one end of color B. Color A will be on harnesses 1 and 3, while color B will be on harnesses 2 and 4.

Start threading at the right-hand side of the loom and work from right to left. Harness 1 is the one closest to you and harness 4 is the last one at the back. After you've finished threading, to be sure that you've threaded correctly, raise harnesses 1 and 3; only color A warp threads should be raised. Raise harnesses 2 and 4; only color B warp threads should be raised.

*Sleying the Reed.* Use the center 8 in (20 cm) on an 8-dent reed. The warp will be sleyed four threads per dent, two ends of color A and 2 ends of color B all across the 8 in (20 cm) of the warp.

## MAKING A SINGLE WARP FOR ALL THE EXERCISES

For those of you who would like to do all the exercises in the book on one warp, I'll give directions for a warp 6 yds (5.5 m) long. As each series of exercises is finished, you can cut off the completed weaving. You can then reattach the warp to the cloth beam before beginning the next series of exercises.

Prepare a warp 6 yd (5.5 m) long according to the following directions:

## For 15 Ends Per Inch in a 15-Dent Reed

Each layer will have 15 ends to the inch (2.5 cm), with 120 ends (15 epi × 8 in or 20 cm) of color A and 120 ends (15 epi × 8 in or 20 cm) of color B, making a total of 240 ends.

120 ends color A × 6 yd (5.5 m) long = 720 yd (655 m) color A warp yarn
120 ends color B × 6 yd (5.5 m) long = 720 yd (655 m) color B warp yarn
For ease in preparing the warp, tie the end of color A yarn and the end of color B yarn together and warp two ends at a time.

*Threading the Loom.* Use a straight threading, 1–2–3–4, alternating one end of color A with one end of color B. Color A will be on harnesses 1 and 3, while color B will be on harnesses 2 and 4. Start threading at the right-hand side of the loom and work from right to left. Harness 1 is the one closest to you at the front and harness 4 is the last one at the back of the loom. After you've finished threading, to be sure that you've threaded correctly, raise harnesses 1 and 3; only color A warp threads should be raised. Raise harnesses 2 and 4; only color B warp threads should be raised.

*Sleying the Reed.* Use the center 8 in (20 cm) on a 15-dent reed. The warp will be sleyed two threads per dent, one thread color A and one thread color B, all across the 8 in (20 cm) of the warp.

## For 16 Ends Per Inch in an Eight-Dent Reed

Each layer will have 16 ends to the inch (2.5 cm) with 128 ends (16 epi × 8 in or 20 cm) of color A and 128 ends (16 epi × 8 in or 20 cm) of color B, making a total of 256 ends.

128 ends color A × 6 yd  (5.5 m) long = 768 yd  (699 m) color A warp yarn
128 ends color B × 6 yd  (5.5 m) long = 768 yd  (699 m) color B warp yarn

For ease in preparing the warp, tie the end of the color A warp yarn and the end of the color B warp yarn together and warp with two ends at a time.

*Threading the Loom.* Use a straight threading, 1–2–3–4, alternating one end of color A with one end of color B. Color A will be on harnesses 1 and 3, while color B will be on harnesses 2 and 4.
   Start threading at the right-hand side of the loom and work from right to left. Harness 1 is the one closest to the front, and harness 4 is the last one at the back of the loom.
   To be sure that you've threaded correctly, raise harnesses 1 and 3; only color A warp threads should be raised. Raise harnesses 2 and 4; only color B warp threads should be raised.

*Sleying the Reed.* Use the center 8 in  (20 cm) on an 8-dent reed. The warp will be sleyed four threads per dent, two ends of color A and two ends of color B, all across the 8 in (20 cm) of the warp.

## Tie-Up For a Jack Loom

The preferred loom to use for these double-weave exercises is one with a rising shed or jack-type loom. For a four-harness jack loom with six treadles, you tie up the end treadle on one side in order to raise all the color A warp threads, which are on harnesses 1 and 3; you tie up the end treadle on the other side in order to raise all the color B warp threads, which are on harnesses 2 and 4. You should also tie up the center four treadles so that each one will cause only one of the four harnesses to be raised, as in a direct tie-up.

The tie-up that will provide the greatest ease in weaving is the one below:

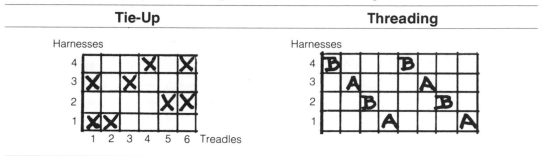

| Tie-Up | Threading |
|--------|-----------|

With this tie-up, your left foot can work the treadles for the color A warp threads and your right foot can work the treadles for the color B warp threads. When all the color A warp ends and half the color B warp ends have to be raised at one time, your left foot can press treadle 1, raising harnesses 1 and 3 (all color A), and at the same time your right foot can press either treadle 4 or 5 to raise either harness 2 or harness 4 (half the color B ends). In the same manner, when all the color B warp ends have to be raised and half the color A warp ends also must be raised, your right foot can press treadle 6 to raise harnesses 2 and 4 (all color B warps), while at the same time your left foot can press either treadle 2 or 3 to raise either harness 1 or harness 3 (half the color A warp ends). If the jack loom has only four treadles for a direct tie-up of only one harness to one treadle, double weave can still be woven. When one harness has to be raised, of course, you press only one treadle. To raise two harnesses, you use both feet, with each one pressing one treadle. To raise three harnesses at one time, you'll learn to use one foot to bridge two treadles and press them down while your other foot presses the third treadle. This procedure may seem awkward at first, but with a little patience and practice, you'll soon become adept at it.

## Tie-Up For a Contremarche Loom

To do all the exercises in this book on a contremarche loom, you would require ten treadles tied up as shown below:

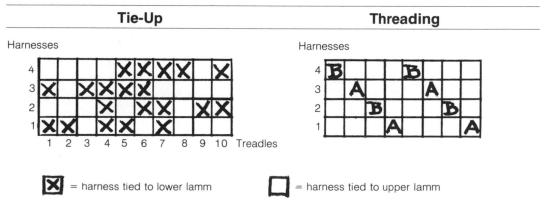

| Tie-Up | Threading |
|--------|-----------|

⊠ = harness tied to lower lamm        ☐ = harness tied to upper lamm

If your contremarche loom does not have ten treadles, you can still do these double-weave exercises. Tie the loom up like a jack-type loom, using only one set of lamms. Use the lower set of lamms, since they are the ones that produce the rising shed on a contremarche loom. Use the tie-up diagram given for the jack loom.

### Tie-Up For a Counterbalanced Loom

You may experience difficulty in weaving double weave on a counterbalanced loom. Some weavers find they can produce a good shed with three harnesses against one on their counterbalanced looms. However, frequently a double shed occurs, making the weaving tedious and subject to errors. If you want to use your counterbalanced loom for double weave, using a shed regulator would be helpful to avoid the double shed and make the weaving go more smoothly.

---

## EXERCISE 1:

# How to Weave Two Separate Layers, With Color A as the Top Layer

---

Now that you've finished threading your loom, all color A threads are on harnesses 1 and 3, while all color B threads are on harnesses 2 and 4. For the weft yarn, you'll need approximately the same amount of yarn you used for the warp. Wind one shuttle with color A and one shuttle with color B.

Before beginning the first exercise, weave about ½ in (1.3 cm) in the following manner, starting with the color A shuttle at the right-hand selvedge and the color B shuttle at the left-hand selvedge:

*Step 1.* Raise harnesses 1 and 2. Weave one shot with color A weft yarn.

*Step 2.* Raise harnesses 3 and 4. Weave one shot with color B weft yarn.

Repeat Steps 1 and 2 three more times. Be sure to interlock the weft threads at the selvedges so that the end threads are woven. In this ½ in (1.3 cm) of weaving, half the color A and half the color B threads are raised for each shot, producing one layer of fabric with the two colors alternating across the width of the fabric. After finishing each exercise, weave ½ in (1.3 cm) in this manner in order to separate the end of one exercise from the beginning of the next.

In Exercise 1, two separate layers will be woven with color A (on harnesses 1 and 3) for the top layer and color B (on harnesses 2 and 4) for the bottom layer. Start weaving with color A shuttle at the right-hand selvedge and color B shuttle at the left-hand selvedge.

*Step 1.* Raise harness 1, which lifts up half the color A warp threads. Weave one shot with color A weft. Lower harness 1.

*Step 2.* Raise harness 3, which lifts up the other half of the color A warp threads. Weave one shot with color A weft, bringing the shuttle back to the right-hand side. Lower harness 3.

These two steps enable you to weave the top layer of fabric with color A warp and weft. In order to weave the bottom layer, all the warp threads of the top layer must be lifted out of the way and alternate halves of the bottom warp threads must be raised.

*Step 3.* Raise harnesses 1 and 3 (all color A warp threads) and also raise harness 2, which lifts up half the color B warp threads. Weave one shot with color B weft. Lower harness 2.

*Step 4.* With harnesses 1 and 3 still up, raise harness 4, which lifts up the other half of the color B warp threads. Weave one shot with color B weft, thus returning the color B shuttle to the left-hand side. Lower harnesses 1, 3, and 4.

Steps 3 and 4 enable you to weave the bottom layer with solid color B warp and weft.

Repeat Steps 1 through 4 for 2 in (5.1 cm). In order to keep the two layers separate, be sure not to cross the weft threads at the selvedges. After weaving 2 in (5.1 cm), raise harnesses 1 and 3. You've now produced two layers of cloth. The top layer, color A warp and weft, is completely separate from the bottom layer, color B warp and weft. If you don't want a solid color fabric, you could, of course, weave the top layer a third color or even wind color B weft on a separate shuttle. In the same way, you could weave the bottom layer with color A weft or a third color. You must weave with two shuttles and be sure to keep the weft threads uncrossed at the selvedges in order to keep the two layers of fabric entirely separate from each other.

Before starting the next exercise, weave ½ in (1.3 cm), alternately raising harnesses 1 and 2 for one shot and harnesses 3 and 4 for the second shot.

---

**EXERCISE 2:**

# How to Weave Two Separate Layers, With Color B as the Top Layer

---

So far we've considered harnesses 1 and 3 with color A warp threads to be the top layer, and harnesses 3 and 4 with color B warp threads to be the bottom layer.

Now we'll reverse the arrangement and assume that you want color B to produce the top layer with color A as the bottom layer. In order to weave the top layer, half the color B warp threads must be raised alternately with the other half of the color B warp threads. In other words, you must alternate harness 2 with harness 4.

*Step 1.* Raise harness 2. Weave one shot with color B weft. Lower harness 2.

*Step 2.* Raise harness 4. Weave one shot with color B weft. Lower harness 4.

Steps 1 and 2 enable you to weave the top layer with solid color B warp and weft. In order to weave the bottom layer, all the warp threads of the top layer (color B on harnesses 2 and 4 ) must be lifted out of the way, and alternate halves of the bottom layer (color A on harnesses 1 and 3) must be raised.

*Step 3.* Raise harnesses 2 and 4 (all color B), and also raise harness 1 (half of the color A warp threads). Weave one shot with color A weft. Lower harness 1.

*Step 4.* With harnesses 2 and 4 still up, raise harness 3, which lifts up the other half of the color A warp threads. Weave one shot with color A weft. Lower harnesses 2, 3, and 4.

Steps 3 and 4 enable you to weave the bottom layer with solid color A warp and weft.

Repeat Steps 1 to 4 for 2 in (5.1 cm). Be sure not to cross the weft threads at the selvedges. Then raise harnesses 2 and 4. You'll see that you've again woven two separate layers. This time, solid color B is on the top and solid color A is on the bottom.

Before starting the next exercise, weave ½ in (1.3 cm) alternately raising harnesses 1 and 2 for one shot and harnesses 3 and 4 for the second shot, ending with color A shuttle at the right-hand selvedge and color B shuttle at the left-hand selvedge.

---

# EXERCISE 3:
# Exchanging the Layers

---

In this exercise, you'll weave separate layers in 1 in (2.5 cm) stripes, with solid color A alternating with solid color B as the top layer. To make the exchange as smooth as possible, the last harness raised for the lower layer should be used for the first shot of the upper layer in the exchange. Thus, if harness 4 is raised for the last shot in weaving, with warp color B as the bottom layer, then harness 4 should be raised for the first weft shot in weaving, with warp color B as the top layer.

### COLOR A AS THE TOP LAYER

*Step 1.* Starting with shuttle color A at the right-hand selvedge, raise harness 1. Weave one shot with color A weft.

*Step 2.* Raise harness 3. Weave one shot with color A weft.

*Step 3.* Raise harnesses 1 and 3 plus 2. Weave one shot with color B weft.

*Step 4.* Raise harnesses 1 and 3 plus 4. Weave one shot with color B weft.

Repeat these four steps for 1 in (2.5 cm). Be sure not to cross the weft threads at the selvedges in order to keep the two layers separate. Solid color A is the top layer, while solid color B is the bottom layer.

## COLOR B AS THE TOP LAYER

*Step 1.* Since harness 4 was the last harness raised for the bottom layer, the transition will be smoother if harness 4 is used first in bringing color B warps to the top layer.

Raise harness 4. Weave one shot with color B weft.

*Step 2.* Raise harness 2. Weave one shot with color B weft.

*Step 3.* Raise harnesses 2 and 4 plus 1. Weave one shot with color A weft.

*Step 4.* Raise harnesses 2 and 4 plus 3. Weave one shot with color A weft.

Repeat these 4 steps for 1 in (2.5 cm).

## COLOR A AGAIN AS THE TOP LAYER

*Step 1.* In order to bring color A warp threads to the top layer again in as smooth a fashion as possible, you should raise harness 3 first, as it was raised in the last shot, with color A as the bottom layer.

Raise harness 3. Weave one shot with color A weft.

*Step 2.* Raise harness 1. Weave one shot with color A weft.

*Step 3.* Raise harnesses 1 and 3 plus 2. Weave one shot with color B weft.

*Step 4.* Raise harnesses 1 and 3 plus 4. Weave one shot with color B weft.

Repeat these four steps for 1 in (2.5 cm). In exchanging the layers, it's sometimes necessary to add two extra shots to the top layer before the exchange. On many looms, the angle of the beater causes the top layer to be more compressed than the bottom layer. When this occurs, the exchange of layers is not as smooth as when the two layers are even. Two extra shots will usually be sufficient to close the gap between the layers.

# EXERCISE 4:
# Brooks Bouquet Lace on the Top Layer With a Solid Bottom Layer

In this exercise, a lace pattern known as *Brooks Bouquet* will be woven on the top layer with a solid-color background woven on the bottom layer. This technique can be used to great advantage in weaving curtains or draperies, evening skirts, or lace wall hangings.

Before starting this exercise, weave ½ in (1.3 cm), alternately raising harnesses 1 and 2 for one shot, and 3 and 4 for the second shot.

*Step 1*. Weave two separate layers for 1 in (2.5 cm), using the four steps of Exercise 1 as follows:

Raise harness 1. Weave one shot witn color A weft.
Raise harness 3. Weave one shot with color A weft.
Raise harnesses 1 and 3 plus 2. Weave one shot with color B weft.
Raise harnesses 1 and 3 plus 4. Weave one shot with color B weft.

Repeat until you've woven 1 in (2.5 cm).

*Step 2*. Raise the top layer out of the way and weave 8 shots with color B warp and weft on the bottom layer as follows:

Raise harnesses 1 and 3 plus 2. Weave one shot with color B weft.
Raise harnesses 1 and 3 plus 4. Weave one shot with color B weft.

Repeat this procedure three more times until you have woven 8 shots with color B weft on the bottom layer. The top layer remains unwoven during Step 2 and will be used for the lace shot in Step 3.

*Step 3*. Weave one row in Brooks Bouquet lace, also called a *backstitch weave* because the weft yarn is wrapped in a backstitching fashion around groups or "bouquets" of warp threads. Raise harness 1 and weave the lace row with color A weft as follows:

Insert the shuttle in the shed going under the first four raised warp threads from right to left, bringing the shuttle out of the shed between the fourth and fifth raised warp threads. Bring the weft yarn back toward the right over the first four raised warps and then back into the shed from right to left under the first eight raised warps, coming out of the shed between the eighth and ninth raised warps.

Pull the weft yarn taut so that the first four threads are grouped together and centered over the first four unraised color A warp threads.

Take the weft yarn back toward the right over four raised warps and back into the shed under eight raised warps. Bring the weft yarn out of the shed at this point and pull threads five through eight into a bouquet as before.

Repeat this process all across the row, each time grouping another four raised warp threads and centering them over the corresponding four unraised color A warps.

When you reach the left-hand selvedge, bring the beater forward, lower harness 1 and raise harness 3. Weave one shot with weft color A, taking care to keep the one area of lace the same above and below the grouping of warp threads.

*Step 4.* Weave two separate layers for ½ in (1.3 cm), using the same procedure as in Step 1 in this exercise.

Repeat Steps 2 through 4 once more. Brooks Bouquet lace could be woven on the upper layer while the bottom layer could be left unwoven for the length of the lace area for a more open or airy feeling for draperies. The two layers could even be woven together as a tabby weave for the areas between the lace.

Before starting the next exercise, weave ½ in (1.3 cm), alternately raising harnesses 1 and 2 for one shot and harnesses 3 and 4 for the second shot.

---

**EXERCISE 5:**

# Leno Lace on the Top Layer With a Solid Bottom Layer

---

In this exercise, another lace pattern, leno lace, will be woven, which could also be used for draperies, lace wall hangings, or evening skirt fabric. Interesting effects can be achieved when harmonious color relationships are established between the top and bottom layers.

*Step 1.* Weave two separate layers for 1 in (2.5 cm), using the four steps of Exercise 1 as follows:

Raise harness 1. Weave one shot with color A weft.
Raise harness 3. Weave one shot with color A weft.
Raise harnesses 1 and 3 plus 2. Weave one shot with color B weft.
Raise harnesses 1 and 3 plus 4. Weave one shot with color B weft.

Repeat until you have woven 1 in (2.5 cm), ending with the color A shuttle at the right-hand side.

*Step 2.* Raise the top layer out of the way and weave 12 shots with color B warp and weft as follows:

Raise harnesses 1 and 3 plus 2. Weave one shot with color B weft.
Raise harnesses 1 and 3 plus 4. Weave one shot with color B weft.

Repeat this procedure five more times until you have woven 12 shots, with color B as the bottom layer. The top layer remains unwoven and will be used for the lace shot in Step 3.

*Step 3.* The leno lace is made with a closed shed using all the color A warp threads. The lace is formed by picking up groups of warp threads and changing their positions in the warp sequence before inserting the weft shot. The inter-changed warp threads are held by a pick-up stick or sword, which is then turned on edge to facilitate the weaving of the weft shot. Leno lace, a gauze weave, has many possible variations, but the lace in this exercise will be worked with groups of four threads. No shed is required, but the tension may be slackened a bit.

The procedure for making the lace is as follows:

Raise all the color A warp threads, harnesses 1 and 3. Pick up the first four color A warps at the right selvedge and bring them to the left over the top of the next four color A warps. Insert the pick-up stick to hold the threads in the exchanged position (Figure 1).

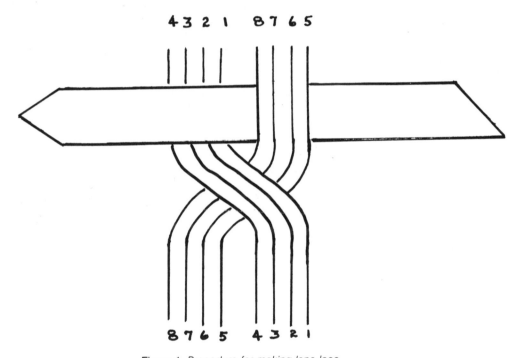

Figure 1. *Procedure for making leno lace.*

Repeat across the row, crossing four threads over the next four threads, right over left, each time moving the stick to hold the exchange. Turn the pick-up stick on edge and weave a shot with color A weft, making sure to keep the weft thread even across the row.

*Step 4.* Keep all color A warp threads raised (harnesses 1 and 3) and weave 12 shots of color B warp and weft, using the same procedure as in Step 2 of this exercise.

*Step 5.* Raise harness 3 and weave one shot of color A weft, bringing that shuttle back to the right-hand side. This shot closes the lace and should leave as much open space above the exchange of the threads as below.

*Step 6.* Weave two separate layers for 1 in (2.5 cm), as outlined in Step 1 of this exercise.

Repeat Steps 2 through 6 of this exercise once more. As with Brooks Bouquet lace, leno lace could be woven on the top layer, while the bottom layer could be left unwoven for a more open feeling for draperies. Here again, the two layers could be interlocked with a tabby weave for the inch (2.5 cm) between the lace areas. Other lace weaves could also be used in this manner, as well as in the endless varieties of both Brooks Bouquet and leno lace.

Before starting the next exercise, weave ½ in (1.3 cm), alternately raising harnesses 1 and 2 for one shot and harnesses 3 and 4 for the second shot, ending with both shuttles at the right-hand selvedge.

# EXERCISE 6:
# How to Weave a Tube With Two Shuttles

In this exercise, you'll weave a tube using two shuttles. One side of the tube will be color A warp and weft and the other side, color B warp and weft. Start with both shuttles at the right-hand side.

*Step 1.* Raise harness 1. Weave one shot with color A weft.

*Step 2.* Raise harnesses 1 and 3 plus 2. Weave one shot with color B weft.

*Step 3.* Raise harness 3. Pick up color A shuttle, pass it under the color B shuttle at the selvedge, and weave one shot with color A weft. By passing one shuttle under the other, an interlocking of the weft threads occurs, closing the tube at the selvedge.

*Step 4.* Raise harnesses 1 and 3 plus 4. Weave one shot with color B weft.

Repeat Steps 1 through 4 for 3 in (7.6 cm), being sure to interlock the weft threads at both the right-hand and left-hand selvedges in order to close the tube at both sides. After you have woven 3 in (7.6 cm), raise harnesses 1 and 3. You will see that you have woven a tube which you may stuff lightly before you close it at the top. Some trial and error may be necessary to determine the correct amount of stuffing used in order to obtain a smooth closing at the top. The closing will occur by weaving the ½ in (1.3 cm) of tabby before the next exercise.

Before starting the next exercise, weave ½ in (1.3 cm), alternately raising harnesses 1 and 2 for one shot and 3 and 4 for the second shot.

# EXERCISE 7:
# How to Weave a Tube With One Shuttle

In this exercise, you'll weave with one shuttle. For the first tube, you'll use the color A shuttle to produce a tube which has a solid color A warp and weft on the top but a color B warp with a color A weft on the bottom. You'll weave the second tube with a solid color B warp and weft on top, but using a color A warp with a color B weft on the bottom.

## TO WEAVE A TUBE WITH COLOR A WARP AND WEFT ON TOP

*Step 1.* Raise harness 1. Weave one shot of color A weft.

*Step 2.* Raise harnesses 1 and 3 plus 2. Weave one shot of color A weft.

*Step 3.* Raise harness 3. Weave one shot of color A weft.

*Step 4.* Raise harnesses 1 and 3 plus 4. Weave one shot of color A weft.

In Steps 1 and 2, you're weaving first across half the threads of the upper layer and then across half the threads of the bottom layer. In Steps 3 and 4, you're weaving across the other half of the threads in the upper layer and then across the other half of the threads of the bottom layer. Since one continuous weft is used, weaving alternately across the top and the bottom layers produces a tube. Repeat Steps 1 through 4 until you've woven 3 in (7.6 cm). Raise harnesses 1 and 3 and stuff the tube lightly.

Weave ½ in (1.3 cm) with color A weft, alternately raising harnesses 1 and 2 for one shot and harnesses 3 and 4 for the second shot. Change to color B weft for the next part of this exercise.

## TO WEAVE A TUBE WITH COLOR B WARP AND WEFT ON TOP

*Step 1.* Raise harness 2. Weave one shot of color B weft.

*Step 2.* Raise harnesses 2 and 4 plus 1. Weave one shot of color B weft.

*Step 3.* Raise harness 4. Weave one shot of color B weft.

*Step 4.* Raise harnesses 2 and 4 plus 3. Weave one shot of color B weft.

Repeat Steps 1 through 4 for 3 in (7.6 cm). Raise harnesses 2 and 4 and stuff the tube lightly.

Weave ½ in (1.3 cm) with color B weft, alternately raising harnesses 1 and 2 for one shot and harnesses 3 and 4 for the seond shot.

Tubular weave is an easy way to make pillows with a minimum of sewing necessary to finish them. In Project 1 at the end of this series of exercises, you'll find directions for a variety of pillows and bags made with a tubular weave.

Tubular weave can also be used for weaving identical pieces of fabric for a plaid weave or a random weft-striped patterned weave. For example, the top layer could be the material for the front of a skirt, while the bottom layer would be for the back of the skirt. Then, when the material is cut for sewing, the plaid or random weft stripes will match exactly. Klara Cherepov has graciously shared this idea with us. This method is so much easier than trying to weave two separate but identical pieces of fabric.

---

# EXERCISE 8:
# How to Weave Two or More Tubes Simultaneously

---

To weave two or more tubes simultaneously, a separate shuttle must be used for each tube you weave. Once you decide which warp threads are to be used for each tube, you must be careful to include only those warps intended for that tube. You must also be careful not to interlock the different weft threads if you want the tubes to remain completely separate from one another. In this exercise, two separate tubes will be woven alongside each other, each using half of the warp threads of each layer. Since the previous exercise ended with the color B weft at the right-hand selvedge, use the color B shuttle to weave the right-hand tube and the color A shuttle for the left-hand tube.

*Step 1.* Raise harnesses 1 and 3. Starting at the right-hand selvedge, count 60 color A warp threads (64, if you started with 128 color A warp ends). Tie a small strand of a different color thread at this point to mark the separation between the tubes.

*Step 2.* Raise harness 1. With the color B weft, weave under the first 30 (or 32) raised warps, going from the right-hand selvedge to the middle. With harness 1 still up, weave, use the color A shuttle to weave under the second 30 (or 32) raised warps, going from the middle to the left-hand selvedge. As an aid in keeping the wefts separate, keep the color B shuttle at the right-hand selvedge between weft shots, and the shuttle with the color A weft at the left-hand selvedge.

*Step 3.* Raise harnesses 1 and 3 plus 2. With the color A weft, weave from the left-hand selvedge to the middle of the warp. With the same harnesses raised, use the color B weft to weave from the middle to the right-hand selvedge.

*Step 4.* Raise harness 3. With the color B weft, weave from the right-hand selvedge to the middle. With the color A weft, weave from the middle to the left selvedge.

*Step 5.* Raise harnesses 1 and 3 plus 4. With the color A weft, weave from the left-hand selvedge to the middle. With the color B weft, weave from the middle to the right-hand selvedge.

Repeat Steps 2 through 5 for approximately 2 in (5.1 cm). The tube on the right has the color A warp and the color B weft on top with the color B warp and weft on the bottom. The tube on the left has the color A warp and weft on top with the color B warp and the color A weft on the bottom. Raise harnesses 1 and 3 and stuff the tubes lightly.

Exchange the layers now and weave with the color B warp as the top layer, but keep the color B weft for the right-hand tube and the color A weft for the left-hand tube.

*Step 6.* Raise harness 4. Weave one shot with the color B weft from the right-hand selvedge to the middle, and one shot of the color A weft from the middle to the left-hand selvedge. Since harness 4 was the harness raised in the last shot before the exchange, a smoother exchange is possible by using harness 4 in this first step.

*Step 7.* Raise harnesses 2 and 4 plus 3. Weave one shot of the color A weft from the left-hand selvedge to the middle, and one shot of the color B weft from the middle to the right-hand selvedge.

*Step 8.* Raise harness 2. Weave with the color B weft from the right-hand selvedge to the middle and with the color A weft from the middle to the left-hand selvedge.

*Step 9.* Raise harnesses 2 and 4 plus 1. With the color A weft, weave from the left-hand selvedge to the middle. With the color B weft, weave from the middle to the right-hand selvedge.

Repeat Steps 6 through 9 for approximately 2 in (5.1 cm).

In weaving, be sure to keep the two weft threads separate from each other and to use the proper warp threads for each tube. Remember, in exchanging the layers, it's sometimes necessary to add two extra shots to the upper layer to compensate for the way the top layer tends to be more compressed by the angle of the beater. Raise harnesses 2 and 4 and stuff each tube lightly. Before starting the next exercise, close the tubes by weaving ½ in (1.3 cm), alternately raising harnesses 1 and 2 for one shot and harnesses 3 and 4 for the second shot.

---

# EXERCISE 9:
# How to Weave Two Tubes Joined at the Exchange of Layers

---

In Exercise 8, you had to be careful to keep the two weft shuttles separate from each other in order to have the two tubes completely separate. In this exercise, you'll keep the tubes separate except at the point where the two layers of warp are exchanged.

*Step 1.* Weave two tubes as in Exercise 8, repeating Steps 2 through 5 for 1 in (2.5 cm).

*Step 2.* Stuff the tubes lightly.

*Step 3.* Exchange the layers by bringing up half the lower warp threads (harness 4). Weave with one shuttle from the right-hand selvedge to the middle. Before weaving with the second shuttle, cross it under the first shuttle so that the weft threads are interlocked. Then weave with the second shuttle from the middle across to the left-hand selvedge.

*Step 4.* Weave with the second shuttle across the bottom of the left-hand tube with harnesses 2 and 4 plus 3 raised. If you wish to continue to have the tubes joined, be sure to take the first shuttle under the second shuttle and then weave across the bottom of the right-hand tube.

After you've joined the tubes at the point of the exchange, you can weave the tubes separately by keeping the two wefts entirely separate just as outlined in Exercise 8.

Bear in mind when weaving tubes that they don't have to be all the same width or the same height. The amount of variation in the size of the tubes is governed by your understanding of which harnesses are producing each layer of each tube and by your patience in the weaving process.

Before weaving the next exercise, weave ½ in (1.3 cm), alternately raising harnesses 1 and 2 for one shot and harnesses 3 and 4 for the second shot.

---

## EXERCISE 10:
# How to Weave a Tube With the Opening on the Right-Hand Side

---

So far, the tubes have been woven with the openings at the top of the tubes. Tubes can also be woven with the openings occurring either at the right-hand or left-hand side. In this exercise, the tubes will be woven with the openings at the right-hand side.

### TO WEAVE A TUBE WITH SOLID COLOR A WARP AND WEFT ON TOP, OPEN AT THE RIGHT

*Step 1.* Raise harness 1. Start with the color A weft at the right-hand selvedge and weave one shot of color A weft.

*Step 2.* Raise harnesses 1 and 3 plus 2. Weave one shot of color A weft.

*Step 3.* Raise harnesses 1 and 3 plus 4. Weave one shot of color A weft.

*Step 4.* Raise harness 3. Weave one shot of color A weft.

Repeat Steps 1 through 4 for 3 in (7.6 cm). In Step 1, the weft yarn goes across half the threads of the upper layer, from right to left. In Step 2, it goes from left to right across half the lower layer, while in Step 3, it comes back from right to left across the other half of the lower warp threads. In Step 4, it then goes from left to right across the second half of the upper layer warp threads. Since the weft thread goes from the top layer to the bottom layer (or vice versa) only at the left-hand selvedge, then the tubular effect occurs only at the left-hand side, leaving the right-hand side open.

If you examine the weaving at the left-hand selvedge, you'll notice that there are two threads lying next to each other in the same warp space. If you were setting up a warp solely for weaving pieces with one side open and one closed, you'd omit the end thread on one of the layers at the selvedge opposite the open side. In other words, if the opening were to occur at the right-hand selvedge, then one end thread would have to be omitted from either the top layer or the bottom layer at the left-hand selvedge.

Before starting the next part of this exercise, weave ½ in (1.3 cm), alternately raising harnesses 1 and 2 for one shot and harnesses 3 and 4 for the second shot.

## TO WEAVE A TUBE WITH COLOR B WARP AND WEFT ON TOP, OPEN AT THE RIGHT

*Step 1.* Raise harness 2. Starting with the color B shuttle at the right-hand selvedge, weave one shot of color B weft.

*Step 2.* Raise harnesses 2 and 4 plus 1. Weave one shot of color B weft.

*Step 3.* Raise harnesses 2 and 4 plus 3. Weave one shot of color B weft.

*Step 4.* Raise harness 4. Weave one shot of color B weft.

Repeat Steps 1 through 4 until you've woven 3 in (7.6 cm). If you raise harnesses 2 and 4, you'll see that you've woven a tube that is open on the right-hand side, with the left-hand side closed. The top is of the solid color B, while the bottom is a mixture of color A warp and color B weft.

Before starting the next exercise, weave ½ in (1.3 cm), alternately raising harnesses 1 and 2 for one shot and harnesses 3 and 4 for the the second shot.

# EXERCISE 11:
# How to Weave a Tube With the Opening on the Left-Hand Side

In this exercise, the opening will occur at the left-hand selvedge. The procedure is much the same as in Exercise 10, but the weaving starts with the color A shuttle at the left-hand side.

## TO WEAVE A TUBE WITH COLOR A WARP AND WEFT ON TOP, OPEN AT THE LEFT

*Step 1.* Raise harness 1. Starting with the color A shuttle at the left selvedge, weave one shot of color A weft.

*Step 2.* Raise harnesses 1 and 3 plus 2. Weave one shot of color A weft.

*Step 3.* Raise harnesses 1 and 3 plus 4. Weave one shot of color A weft.

*Step 4.* Raise harness 3. Weave one shot of color A weft.

Repeat Steps 1 through 4 for 3 in (7.6 cm). In Step 1, the weft goes from left to right over half the upper warp threads. Step 2 goes from right to left over half the lower warp threads, while Step 3 goes from left to right over the other half of the lower warp. Step 4 brings the weft thread back to the top from right to left across the other half of the upper layer warp threads. Since the weft thread goes from the top layer to the bottom layer (or vice versa) only at the right-hand selvedge, the tubular effect occurs only at the right-hand side, leaving the left-hand side open. If you raise harnesses 1 and 3, you'll see that you're weaving with the left-hand side open.

Weave ½ in (1.3 cm) with color A weft, alternately raising harnesses 1 and 2 for one shot and harnesses 3 and 4 for the second shot. Change to the shuttle with color B weft.

## TO WEAVE A TUBE WITH COLOR B WARP AND WEFT ON TOP, OPEN AT THE LEFT

*Step 1.* Raise harness 2. Start with the color B weft shuttle at the left selvedge and weave one shot of color B weft.

*Step 2.* Raise harnesses 2 and 4 plus 1. Weave one shot of color B weft.

*Step 3.* Raise harnesses 2 and 4 plus 3. Weave one shot of color B weft.

*Step 4.* Raise harness 4. Weave one shot of color B weft.

Repeat Steps 1 through 4 until you've woven 3 in (7.6 cm). Then raise harnesses 2 and 4 and you'll see that you're weaving with the opening at the left-hand side. The top is now color B warp and weft, while the bottom is a mixture of color A warp and color B weft.

The procedures outlined in both Exercises 10 and 11 can be used to produce double-width fabric. In this way, a loom with a weaving width of 20 in (51 cm) can be used to weave a fabric which starts out 40 in (102 cm) wide in the warp. The weaving will be limited to plain or tabby weave, because only two harnesses are available for each layer of the weaving. Interesting plaids can be woven by warping with a series of colors in varying widths, and then weaving with two or more weft colors in stripes of various sizes.

To minimize the effect of drawing in at the fold, you can sley the warp more openly at the selvedge where the fold will occur. If the open side is to be at the right, with the fold or closed side at the left, then the warp would be set more openly at the left-hand selvedge. For example, if the warp is sleyed two threads per dent across the rest of the warp, then the last two threads on each layer at the left-hand selvedge could be set at only one thread per dent. Another way to offset the effect of drawing in at the fold is to place a color change at the point, thus drawing attention to the colors rather than to the fold.

*Note:* Most weavers produce one selvedge that is better than the other. Usually a right-handed person will have a more even left-hand selvedge, while a left-handed person usually makes a better right-hand selvedge. Notice if this is true in your weaving, as it may be a factor in deciding whether or not to have a right-hand or left-hand opening when you are weaving tubes, pillows, or double-width fabric.

Before starting the next exercise, weave ½ in (1.3 cm), alternately raising harnesses 1 and 2 for one shot and harnesses 3 and 4 for the second shot.

---

## EXERCISE 12:
# How to Weave a Tube With the Opening in the Middle of the Top Layer

---

Before starting the weaving, mark the center of the color A warp threads (the top layer). Start with the shuttle with the color A weft at the right-hand selvedge.

*Step 1.* Raise harness 1. Weave with color A weft from the right-hand selvedge to the middle of the warp.

*Step 2.* Raise harness 3. Weave with color A weft from the middle of the warp back to the right-hand selvedge.

*Step 3.* Raise harnesses 1 and 3 plus 2. Weave with color A weft from the right-hand to the left-hand selvedge.

*Step 4.* Raise harness 1. Weave with color A weft from the left-hand selvedge to the middle of the warp.

*Step 5.* Raise harness 3. Weave with color A from the middle of the warp back to the left-hand selvedge.

*Step 6.* Raise harnesses 1 and 3 plus 4. Weave with color A from the left-hand selvedge across to the right-hand selvedge.

Repeat Steps 1 through 6 for 3 in (7.6 cm). As this warp has been set up, you've woven color A warp and weft on top with a mixture of colors A and B on the bottom. By weaving with color B weft and using harnesses 2 and 4 for the top layer, you can weave solid color B as the top layer with a mixture of colors B and A on the lower layer.

The procedure of Exercise 12 can be used for pillows requiring very little sewing. By closing the tube at the top and the bottom, you need only insert a pillow stuffing through the slit, and then sew up the slit.

To end this series of exercises, weave ½ in (1.3 cm), alternately raising harnesses 1 and 2 for one shot and harnesses 3 and 4 for the second shot.

On the pages that follow, I'll give suggestions for making projects utilizing the techniques covered in this group of exercises. To review briefly, we've produced fabrics made up of two layers that have remained completely separate from each other and have alternated as the top and the bottom layers. Lace weaves have been introduced on one layer, while the other layer was woven in plain weave to serve as a background for the lace. Tubular weaving has been explored to produce tubes open at the top or the bottom or at either side, and to produce multiple tubes across the width of the fabric. By weaving two layers of cloth, joined at one side but open at the other, you can get a double-width fabric and thus expand the capabilities of even narrow-width looms. I'll provide specific directions for some projects; you'll find additional ideas in the photographs that appear in this book.

# PROJECT 1:

# Four Styles of Tubular Pillows Plus One Shoulder Bag and One Saddle Bag on a 6-yd (5.5-m) Warp

This project is based on one designed and woven by Judy Spark at the College of New Rochelle in New York. For both warp and weft she used Marks Tunagarn, a two-ply Swedish wool from Ulltex, in three shades of green. The warp sett was 12 ends per inch (2.5 cm) for each layer, two threads per dent (one from each layer) in a 12-dent reed. In her warp, Judy arranged the three colors in an uneven plaid design, with the lower layer the reverse of the upper layer.

In the plaid design for this project, the three colors are arranged in a more balanced plaid; the location of the dark green remains the same on the top and bottom layers, while the medium and light greens exchange places with each other on the bottom layer.

## MAKING THE WARP

In the directions given below, the colors are designated as follows: dark green = DG, medium green = MG, light green = LG. (Of course, you can substitute any other color you like and still use this same plaid design.)

| Top Layer (see Figure 2) | | | | | | | | | | | | | | |
|---|---|---|---|---|---|---|---|---|---|---|---|---|---|---|
| Color | DG | MG | LG | MG | DG | LG | DG | MG | DG | LG | DG | MG | LG | MG | DG |
| Number of Ends | 24 | 6 | 12 | 12 | 6 | 15 | 12 | 6 | 12 | 15 | 6 | 12 | 12 | 6 | 24 |

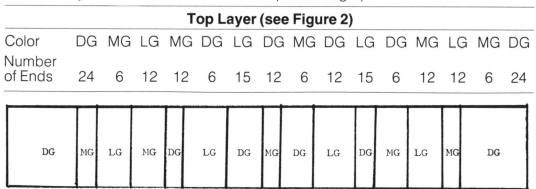

Figure 2. *The top layer of the warp.*

| Bottom Layer (see Figure 3) | | | | | | | | | | | | | | |
|---|---|---|---|---|---|---|---|---|---|---|---|---|---|---|---|
| Color | DG | LG | MG | LG | DG | MG | DG | LG | DG | MG | DG | LG | MG | LG | DG |
| Number of Ends | 24 | 6 | 12 | 12 | 6 | 15 | 12 | 6 | 12 | 15 | 6 | 12 | 12 | 6 | 24 |

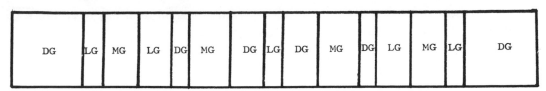

Figure 3. *The bottom layer of the warp.*

There are a total of 180 ends for each layer at 12 ends per inch for a warp 15 in (38 cm) wide. The amount of warp yarn yardage needed of each color is determined by adding the total number of ends for each color and then multiplying by the length of the warp.

Dark Green. 84 ends per layer × 2 = 168 ends × 6 yd (5.5 m) = 1008 warp yd
Medium Green. 42 ends on top + 54 on bottom = 96 ends × 6 yd (5.5 m) = 576 warp yd
Light Green. 54 ends on top + 42 on bottom = 96 ends × 6 yd (5.5 m) = 576 warp yd needed for this color

Assuming that approximately the same amount of each color will be used for the weft as was used for the warp, the following yardage of yarn will be needed for each color:

| | |
|---|---|
| Dark Green | 2016 yd (1835 m) |
| Medium Green | 1152 yd (1048 m) |
| Light Green | 1152 yd (1048 m) |

Each skein of Tunagarn contains approximately 361 yd (320 m); therefore six skeins of dark green are needed for this project, four skeins of medium green, and four skeins of light green. Although you may not choose to use this same yarn for your project, these calculations will serve as a guide in figuring how much yarn you should purchase.

After you've made your warp, thread the loom on a straight threading, 1–2–3–4, with the upper layer on harnesses 1 and 3 and the lower layer on harnesses 2 and 4. With this warp set up as a plaid, there will be stripes of all three colors appearing on each layer. Once you've threaded your warp, raise harnesses 1 and 3 and count each color group to see that you have the correct number of ends for each stripe of the upper layer. Then raise harnesses 2 and 4 and do the same for the bottom layer.

Use the center 15 in (38 cm) of a 12-dent reed. The warp will be sleyed two ends per dent. If you have a tendency to draw in too much at the selvedges, you may elect to sley more openly at the selvedges by sleying the first two threads of each layer singly at both the right-hand and the left-hand selvedges.

## TO WEAVE A PILLOW WITH A CLOSED HEM AT THE BOTTOM AND TWO LAYERS FOR THE HEM AT THE TOP

*Step 1.* To make the closed hem at the bottom, weave 1 in (2.5 cm) by alternately raising harnesses 1 and 2 for one shot and harnesses 3 and 4 for the second shot. Weave with one shuttle wound with dark green weft.

*Step 2.* To make the body of the square pillow, weave a tube for approximately 15 in (38 cm), using the four steps given below:

Raise harness 1. Weave one shot.
Raise harnesses 1 and 3 plus 2. Weave one shot.
Raise harness 3. Weave one shot.
Raise harnesses 1 and 3 plus 4. Weave one shot.

Use one shuttle at a time, following the color sequence of the plaid design on the top warp layer as follows:

| Color of the Weft | Amount to be Woven |
|:---:|:---:|
| DG | 2 in (5.1 cm) |
| MG | ½ in (1.3 cm) |
| LG | 1 in (2.5 cm) |
| MG | 1 in (2.5 cm) |
| DG | ½ in (1.3 cm) |
| LG | 1¼ in (3.2 cm) |
| DG | 1 in (2.5 cm) |
| MG | ½ in (1.3 cm) |
| DG | 1 in (2.5 cm) |
| LG | 1¼ in (3.2 cm) |
| DG | ½ in (1.3 cm) |
| MG | 1 in (2.5 cm) |
| LG | 1 in (2.5 cm) |
| MG | ½ in (1.3 cm) |
| DG | 2 in (5.1 cm) |

*Step 3.* To make the hem at the top, weave two separate layers for 1 in (2.5 cm), with two shuttles wound with dark green weft as follows:

Shuttle A. Raise harness 1. Weave one shot.
Shuttle A. Raise harness 3. Weave one shot.
Shuttle B. Raise harnesses 1 and 3 plus 2. Weave one shot.
Shuttle B. Raise harnesses 1 and 3 plus 4. Weave one shot.

Be sure to keep the weft threads uncrossed at the selvedges so that the two layers remain separate.

Step 3 completes the weaving for the first pillow. Weave 1 in (2.5 cm) in a different color before starting the weaving for the next pillow. All the pillows and bags can be woven before removing any of them from the loom.

   To finish the pillow, when the completed weaving is taken off the loom, cut the fabric at the *top* of the two separate layers. Turn the pillow inside out so that the hem woven in Step 1 is inside and a smooth closed bottom is outside. At the top, there are two separate 1-in (2.5-cm) layers to be folded down inside to allow for attaching a zipper or other closure. With that done, the pillow stuffing can be inserted and the pillow is finished.

*Note:* It is assumed that you'll steam press your fabric before finishing the pillows.

## TO WEAVE A FRINGED PILLOW CLOSED AT TOP AND BOTTOM, OPEN AT THE RIGHT

*Step 1.* To weave a closed bottom, first leave 4 in (10.2 cm) of warp (or more if you wish) unwoven to allow for the fringe at the bottom; then weave ½ in (1.3 cm) with the dark green weft, alternately raising harnesses 1 and 2 for one shot and harnesses 3 and 4 for the second shot. End with the shuttle at the right-hand selvedge.

*Step 2.* To weave the tube with the opening at the right-hand selvedge, weave approximately 15 in (38 cm), using the four steps given below:

Raise harness 1. Weave one shot.
Raise harnesses 1 and 3 plus 2. Weave one shot.
Raise harnesses 1 and 3 plus 4. Weave one shot.
Raise harness 3. Weave one shot.

Use one shuttle at a time, following the color sequence of the plaid design on the bottom layer as given below:

| Color of the Weft | Amount to be Woven |
|:---:|:---:|
| DG | 2 in (5.1 cm) |
| LG | ½ in (1.3 cm) |
| MG | 1 in (2.5 cm) |
| LG | 1 in (2.5 cm) |
| DG | ½ in (1.3 cm) |
| MG | 1¼ in (3.2 cm) |
| DG | 1 in (2.5 cm) |
| LG | ½ in (1.3 cm) |
| DG | 1 in (2.5 cm) |
| MG | 1¼ in (3.2 cm) |
| DG | ½ in (1.3 cm) |
| MG | 1 in (2.5 cm) |
| LG | 1 in (2.5 cm) |
| MG | ½ in (1.3 cm) |
| DG | 2 in (5 cm) |

*Step 3.* To make the closed hem at the top, weave ½ in (1.3 cm) with the dark green weft, alternately raising harnesses 1 and 2 for one shot and harnesses 3 and 4 for the second shot. After you've woven this ½ in (1.3 cm), leave 4 in (10 cm) of warp (or more) unwoven for the fringe at the top.

Step 3 completes the weaving for this pillow. Before starting the next pillow, weave 1 in (2.5 cm) in a different color.

To finish the pillow, when the weaving is taken off the loom, cut the fabric at the *top* of the fringe left for the top of the pillow. Cut off the separating strip which you wove in a different color between the first and second pillows. Now the bottom fringe is free. If you wish, you may attach a zipper at the right-hand selvedge. Or you can insert the pillow stuffing through the opening and then carefully hand-sew the two selvedges together, using the dark green thread to match the color occurring at the selvedges. The fringe may be knotted if you wish; knotting the two layers of fringe together at the top and at the bottom is sufficient to create a closed top and bottom without the weaving done in Steps 1 and 3.

## TO WEAVE A TUBULAR PILLOW, FRINGED AND CLOSED AT THE TOP AND BOTTOM, WITH A SMALL OPENING AT THE MIDDLE LEFT

*Step 1.* Leave 4 in (10 cm) or more of warp unwoven to allow for fringe. To close the bottom, weave ½ in (1.3 cm) with dark green weft, alternately raising harnesses 1 and 2 for one shot and harnesses 3 and 4 for the second shot, ending with the shuttle at the left-hand selvedge. If you are going to knot the fringe when finishing the pillow, you may elect to omit this ½ in (1.3 cm) of weaving.

*Step 2.* Starting with the weft at the left-hand selvedge, weave 5 in (12.7 cm) in tubular weave as follows:

Raise harness 1. Weave one shot.
Raise harnesses 1 and 3 plus 2. Weave one shot.
Raise harness 3. Weave one shot.
Raise harnesses 1 and 3 plus 4. Weave one shot.

Use one shuttle at a time, following the first 5 in (12.7 cm) of the color sequence of the top layer.

| Color of the Weft | Amount to be Woven |
|:---:|:---:|
| DG | 2 in (5 cm) |
| MG | ½ in (1.3 cm) |
| LG | 1 in (2.5 cm) |
| MG | 1 in (2.5 cm) |
| DG | ½ in (1.3 cm) |

*Step 3.* Weave double-width fabric for 5 in (12.7 cm), with the opening at the left-hand selvedge, as follows:

Raise harness 1. With the shuttle starting at the left selvedge, weave one shot.
Raise harnesses 1 and 3 plus 2. Weave one shot.
Raise harnesses 1 and 3 plus 4. Weave one shot.
Raise harness 3. Weave one shot.

Use one shuttle at a time in the color sequence of the center 5 in (12.7 cm) of the top warp layer.

| Color of the Weft | Amount to be Woven |
|:---:|:---:|
| LG | 1¼ in (3.2 cm) |
| DG | 1 in (2.5 cm) |
| MG | ½ in (1.3 cm) |
| DG | 1 in (2.5 cm) |
| LG | 1¼ in (3.2 cm) |

*Step 4.* Step 4 follows the same treadling as Step 2 to weave a tube for 5 in (12.7 cm). Use one shuttle at a time, following the color sequence of the last 5 in (12.7 cm) of the top warp layer.

| Color of the Weft | Amount to be Woven |
|---|---|
| DG | ½ in (1.3 cm) |
| MG | 1 in (2.5 cm) |
| LG | 1 in (2.5 cm) |
| MG | ½ in (1.3 cm) |
| DG | 2 in (5.1 cm) |

*Step 5.* To close the top hem, weave ½ in (1.3 cm) with dark green weft, alternately raising harnesses 1 and 2 for one shot and harnesses 3 and 4 for the other shot. Leave 4 in (10 cm) or more of warp unwoven to allow for fringe. If you are going to knot the fringe together at the top, you may elect to omit this ½ in (1.3 cm) of weaving.

Step 5 completes the weaving for this pillow. Before starting the weaving for the next pillow, weave 1 in (2.5 cm) in a different color.

To finish the pillow, when the finished weaving is taken off the loom, cut the fabric at the *top* of the fringe left for the top of the pillow. Trim off the separating strip woven in a different color below the bottom fringe of the pillow. If you're going to knot the fringe, be sure to push the knots up very close to the last row of the weaving for the pillow. To keep the closing smooth, use small groups of warp ends for each knot.

For the pillow stuffing, make a muslin tube the size of the pillow with a 5 in (12.7 cm) opening on the left-hand side. Insert the muslin tube through the opening in the woven pillow and place the correct amount of stuffing material into the muslin tube. Sew up the slit in the muslin tube and then hand-sew the slit in the woven pillow using the dark green weft to match the color at the selvedges. The pillow is now finished.

## TO WEAVE A PILLOW WITH A SLIT
## IN THE MIDDLE OF THE TOP LAYER

*Step 1.* To make the closed hem at the bottom, weave 1 in (2.5 cm) with dark green weft, alternately raising harnesses 1 and 2 for the first shot and harnesses 3 and 4 for the second shot.

*Step 2.* Weave a slit in the top layer with the bottom layer solid by weaving approximately 15 in (38 cm), using the treadling sequence given below:

Raise harness 1. Start at the right selvedge and weave one shot to the middle of the raised top-layer warp threads, the middle of the center medium green stripe.
Raise harness 3. Weave one shot going from the middle to the right-hand selvedge.
Raise harnesses 1 and 3 plus 2. Weave one shot all across from the right-hand to the left-hand selvedge.

Raise harness 1. Weave one shot from the left-hand selvedge to the middle of the raised warp threads.

Raise harness 3. Weave one shot from the middle, back to the left selvedge.

Raise harnesses 1 and 3 plus 4. Weave one shot all across from the left-hand to the right-hand selvedge.

Use one shuttle at a time, following the color sequence of the plaid design of the bottom layer as given below:

| Color of the Weft | Amount to be Woven |
|:---:|:---:|
| DG | 2 in (5.1 cm) |
| LG | ½ in (1.3 cm) |
| MG | 1 in (2.5 cm) |
| LG | 1 in (2.5 cm) |
| DG | ½ in (1.3 cm) |
| MG | 1¼ in (3.2 cm) |
| DG | 1 in (2.5 cm) |
| LG | ½ in (1.3 cm) |
| DG | 1 in (2.5 cm) |
| MG | 1¼ in (3.2 cm) |
| DG | ½ in (1.3 cm) |
| MG | 1 in (2.5 cm) |
| LG | 1 in (2.5 cm) |
| MG | ½ in (1.3 cm) |
| DG | 2 in (5.1 cm) |

*Step 3.* To weave the closed top, weave 1 in (2.5 cm) with the dark green weft, alternately raising harnesses 1 and 2 for one shot and harnesses 3 and 4 for the second shot.

Step 3 finishes the weaving for this pillow. Before starting the weaving for the shoulder bag, weave 1 in (2.5 cm) in a different color.

To finish the pillow, cut the fabric at the *top* of the 1-in (2.5-cm) strip woven for the top hem. Cut off the separating strip woven below the 1-in (2.5-cm) hem for the bottom of the pillow. Turn the pillow completely inside out so the two woven hem strips are inside the pillow. There are now smooth finished edges at both the top and the bottom of the pillow. Insert a pillow stuffing through the slit on the top layer. Hand-sew the two edges of the slit together with the medium green weft to match the warp stripe. The pillow is now finished. You could, of course, attach a zipper or other closure to the edges of the slit, if you did not want to sew them together.

## TO WEAVE A TUBULAR SHOULDER BAG

The shoulder bag will measure approximately 14 in (35.6 cm) square when it is finished. If you use a strong, tightly woven fabric for the lining, you will have a roomy and very serviceable tote bag.

*Step 1.* To weave the closed hem at the bottom of the bag, weave 1 in (2.5 cm) with one shuttle by alternately raising harnesses 1 and 2 for one shot and harnesses 3 and 4 for the second shot.

*Step 2.* To weave the body of the bag, using one shuttle, weave a 14-in (35.6-cm) tube as follows:

Raise harness 1. Weave one shot.
Raise harnesses 1 and 3 plus 2. Weave one shot.
Raise harness 3. Weave one shot.
Raise harnesses 1 and 3 plus 4. Weave one shot.

*Step 3.* To weave a hem at the top, weave two separate layers for 2 in (5.1 cm), using two shuttles, as follows:

Shuttle A. Raise harness 1. Weave one shot.
Shuttle A. Raise harness 3. Weave one shot.
Shuttle B. Raise harnesses 1 and 3 plus 2. Weave one shot.
Shuttle B. Raise harnesses 1 and 3 plus 4. Weave one shot.

Be sure to keep the weft threads separate at the selvedges in order to keep the two layers separate.

Step 3 completes the weaving for the shoulder bag. No color sequence has been given, but you could use the same arrangement as is found in either the top layer plaid or the bottom layer plaid. You could also choose to weave it all in one color or any combination that suits your fancy. Before starting the weaving for the saddle bag, weave 1 in (2.5 cm) in a different color.

To finish the bag, after the weaving is taken off the loom, cut the fabric above the 2 in (5.1 cm) woven for the hems at the top. At the bottom, cut off the 1-in (2.5-cm) separating strip. Turn the bag completely inside out so that the 1 in (2.5 cm) woven for the bottom hem is now inside the bag and there is a smooth finished edge at the bottom. Use the 2 in (5.1 cm) woven at the top to make hems for the two sides of the top.

If you leave the side selvedges of the hems open at each side, you can insert cords to use as drawstrings for the top of the bag. You might use interesting braids as the cords; they could even be made long enough to serve as shoulder straps. Or you might choose to put a zipper at the top of the bag and sew shoulder straps on the outside of the bag, running down each side. The bag could also be woven with a fringe allowance at the bottom; in this case, the bag need not be turned inside out in the finishing.

## TO WEAVE A SADDLE BAG IN TUBULAR WEAVE

The saddle bag will have two compartments, separated by a single-layer woven strip that will serve as the handle of the bag. Each compartment will measure approximately 14 in (35.6 cm) square; the single-layer woven strip will be 14 in (35.6 cm) long (see Figure 4).

*Step 1.* To weave the closed hem at the bottom of the first compartment, weave 1 in (2.5 cm) with one shuttle, alternately raising harnesses 1 and 2 for one shot and harnesses 3 and 4 for the second shot.

**Figure 4.** *To weave the saddle bag:*

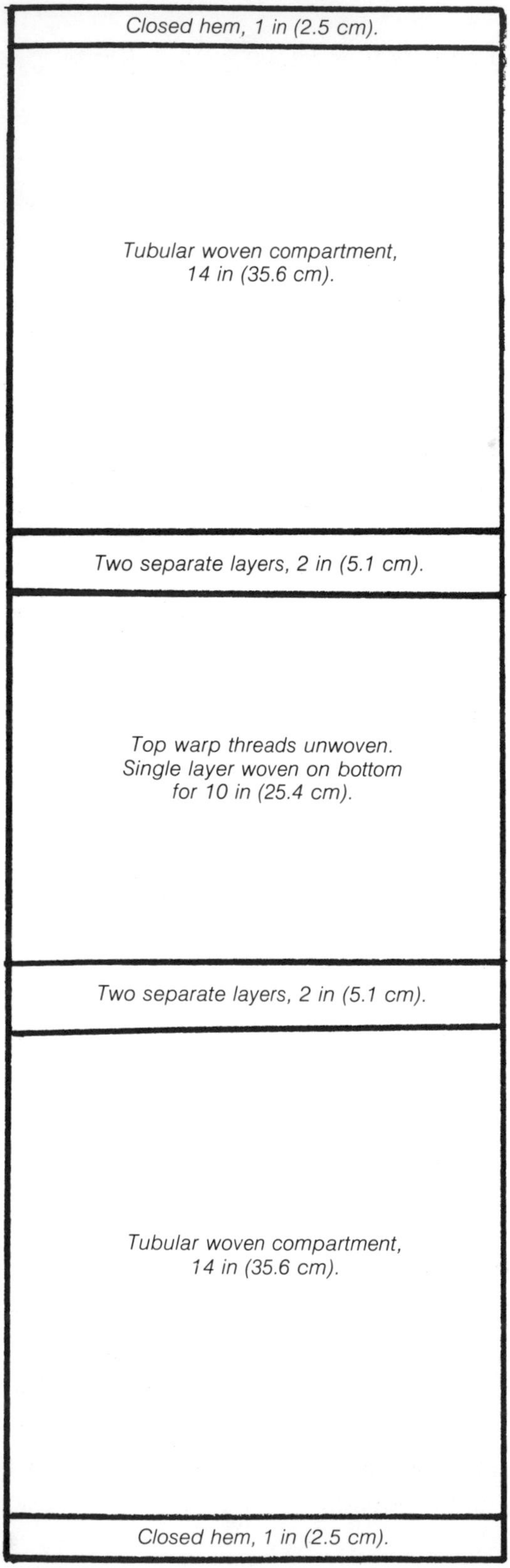

| |
|---|
| Closed hem, 1 in (2.5 cm). |
| Tubular woven compartment, 14 in (35.6 cm). |
| Two separate layers, 2 in (5.1 cm). |
| Top warp threads unwoven. Single layer woven on bottom for 10 in (25.4 cm). |
| Two separate layers, 2 in (5.1 cm). |
| Tubular woven compartment, 14 in (35.6 cm). |
| Closed hem, 1 in (2.5 cm). |

**Figure 5.** *To finish the saddle bag:*

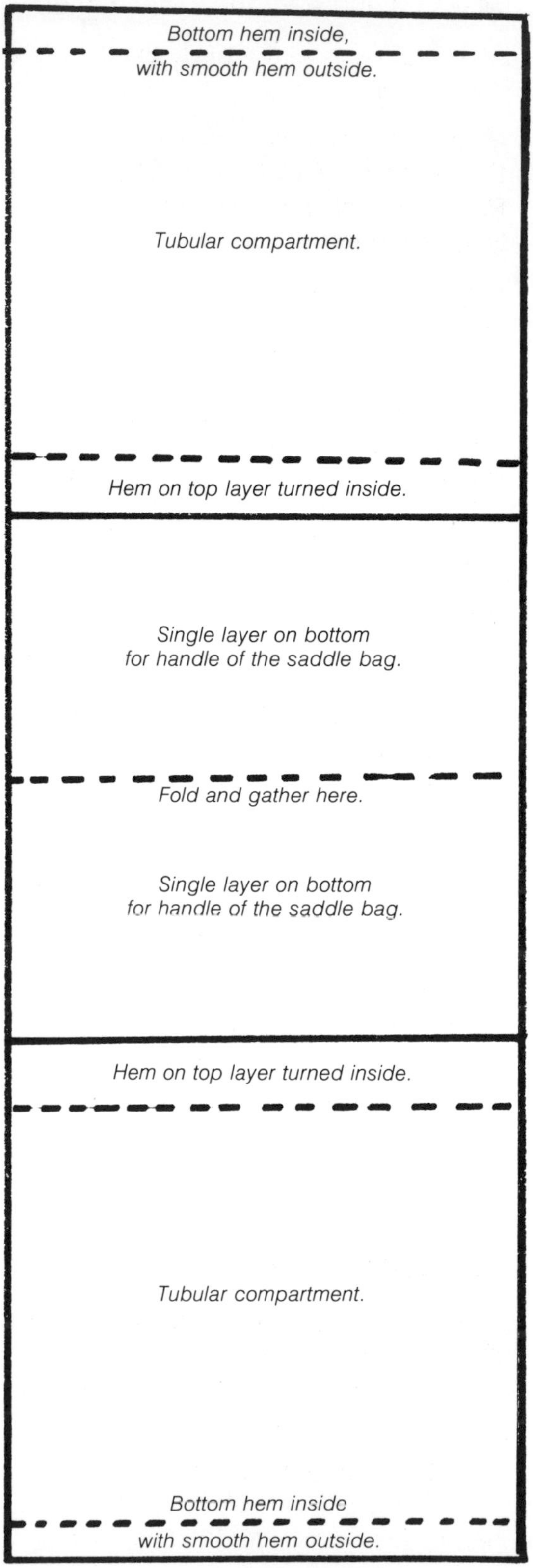

| |
|---|
| Bottom hem inside, with smooth hem outside. |
| Tubular compartment. |
| Hem on top layer turned inside. |
| Single layer on bottom for handle of the saddle bag. |
| Fold and gather here. |
| Single layer on bottom for handle of the saddle bag. |
| Hem on top layer turned inside. |
| Tubular compartment. |
| Bottom hem inside with smooth hem outside. |

*Step 2.* With one shuttle, weave a 14-in (35.6-cm) tube for the body of the compartment, as follows:

Raise harness 1. Weave one shot.
Raise harnesses 1 and 3 plus 2. Weave one shot.
Raise harness 3. Weave one shot.
Raise harnesses 1 and 3 plus 4. Weave one shot.

*Step 3.* To weave a hem on the top layer and the beginning of the single-layer strip on the bottom, use two shuttles. Weave 2 in (5.1 cm), as follows:

Shuttle A. Raise harness 1. Weave one shot.
Shuttle A. Raise harness 3. Weave one shot.
Shuttle B. Raise harnesses 1 and 3 plus 2. Weave one shot.
Shuttle B. Raise harnesses 1 and 3 plus 4. Weave one shot.

Be sure to keep the weft threads separate at the selvedges.

*Step 4.* To continue weaving the strip on the bottom layer, weave with Shuttle B for another 10 in (25 cm). Use the two treadlings for Shuttle B in Step 3. The top warp threads are not woven in Step 4.

*Step 5.* To weave a hem for the top layer of the second compartment and to finish the single-layer strip on the bottom layer, weave 2 in (5.1 cm) according to the complete sequence of Step 3. The single-layer strip on the bottom layer should now measure 14 in (35.6 cm) long.

*Step 6.* To weave the body of the second compartment, weave a 14-in (35.6-cm) tube, following the directions in Step 2.

*Step 7.* To weave the closed hem at the bottom of the second compartment, weave 1 in (2.5 cm) with one shuttle, alternately raising harnesses 1 and 2 for one shot and harnesses 3 and 4 for the second shot.

Step 7 completes the weaving for the saddle bag, the last piece to be woven for Project 1. You may choose your own weft colors for this bag.

To finish the saddle bag (see Figure 5), when the fabric is taken off the loom, cut off the separating strip below the 1-in (2.5-cm) hem at the bottom of the first compartment. Cut off the floating top-layer warp threads, leaving the two woven 1-in (2.5-cm) hems intact. Turn the two compartments completely inside out so that each bottom hem is inside. There is now a smooth, finished bottom on each of the two tubes. Turn the two 1-in (2.5-cm) strips inside to make a hem for the top of the upper layer of each tube.

With the open side of the compartments facing up, fold the weaving at the midpoint of the center single-layer strip. Using the same yarn as was used for the weft, sew several rows in a running stitch at this midpoint; now gather the running stitches up tight until the fabric is about 4 in (10.2 cm) wide and knot the stitches securely. The center strip has become a handle to be placed over your wrist when carrying your saddle bag. The bag could also be placed over a bar at the side of your loom as a handy way to keep shuttles and other small weaving equipment.

# A Ruana-Styled Poncho and a Bog Shirt in Double Weave on an 18-in (45.7-cm)-Wide Warp

The inspiration for this project comes from one designed and woven by Eileen Caruso at the College of New Rochelle. Weaving clothing can be fun, especially if you can produce a ruana-styled poncho and a bog shirt on a warp only 18 in (45.7 cm) wide. Eileen chose for her project Marks Homespun, a soft medium-weight singles woolen yarn from Ulltex. The bulk of her warp was in one color, with narrow bands of two related colors at each end of both the top and the bottom layers. A warp 6 yd (5.5 m) long is ample to complete the two garments which require very little in the way of finishing. The warp sett was eight ends to the inch (2.5 cm) for each layer, two ends per dent in an eight-dent reed.

## MAKING THE WARP

Both the top and the bottom layers will have the colors arranged in the following order (see Figure 6):

| Color A | Color B | Color C | Color A | Color B | Color C | Color B |
|---------|---------|---------|---------|---------|---------|---------|
| 1 in (2.5 cm) 8 ends | 1 in (2.5 cm) 8 ends | 12½ in (31.8 cm) 100 ends | 1 in (2.5 cm) 8 ends | 1 in (2.5 cm) 8 ends | 1 in (2.5 cm) 8 ends | ½ in (1.3 cm) 3 ends on top 4 ends on bottom |

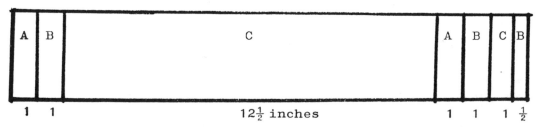

Figure 6. *The warp for Project 2. Both the top and the bottom layers have the same warp arrangement.*

Notice that the ½ in (1.3 cm) of color B at the right-hand selvedge omits one thread on the upper layer to avoid having two threads in the same space when weaving part of the project as double-width fabric.

To figure the amount of yarn needed for the warp, add the total number of ends for both layers and multiply by the length of the warp:

Color A. 32 ends × 6 yd  (5.5 m) = 192 yd  (174.7 m)
Color B. 39 ends × 6 yd  (5.5 m) = 234 yd  (213 m)
Color C. 216 ends × 6 yd  (5.5 m) = 1296 yd  (1179.4 m)

Because the weft stripes are identical with the warp stripes and the weaving is produced as a balanced weave, approximately as much of each color will be needed for the weft as was allowed for the warp. Therefore the total amount of yarn needed for the project is as follows:

Color A for warp and weft          384 yd (349.4 m)
Color B for warp and weft          468 yd (405.9 m)
Color C for warp and weft         2592 yd (2358.7 m)

Each tube of Marks Homespun contains 274 yd (249.3 m). For the project, two tubes each are needed for both color A and color B; and ten tubes are needed of color C. Of course, you may choose an entirely different yarn for the project, but these calculations can serve as a guide in figuring how much yarn to purchase.

When placing the warp on the warping mill or warping board, the threads will be in the order given below:

16 A       16 B       200 C       16 A       16 B       16 C       7 B

Thread the warp on a straight threading, 1–2–3–4, with the top layer on harnesses 1 and 3 and the bottom layer on harnesses 2 and 4. The warp should be threaded on the loom with the 16 ends of colors A and B at the left-hand selvedge and the 16 A, 16 B, 16 C, and 7 B at the right-hand selvedge. To sley the warp, use the center 18 in (45.7 cm) of an eight-dent reed. Sley the warp two ends per dent except at the right-hand selvedge, where the end thread will be alone in one dent.

## TO WEAVE A RUANA-STYLED PONCHO

The poncho is woven using two double-weave techniques, double width for one half and two separate layers for the other half. The double-width cloth is the back of the poncho, approximately 36 in (91.4 cm) wide; the two separate layers are the two sides of the front, each about 18 in (45.7 cm) wide. The directions given are for a poncho 31 in (78.7 cm) long, from the shoulder to the mid-thigh area (see Figure 7).

*Step 1.* Weave the back of the poncho in double-width fabric, with the fold at the right-hand selvedge. Start with the shuttle at the left-hand selvedge, and use the treadling sequence below:

Raise harness 1. Weave one shot from left to right on the top layer.
Raise harnesses 1 and 3 plus 2. Weave one shot from right to left on the bottom layer.
Raise harnesses 1 and 3 plus 4. Weave one shot from left to right on the bottom layer.

**Figure 7.** *To weave the ruana-styled poncho:*

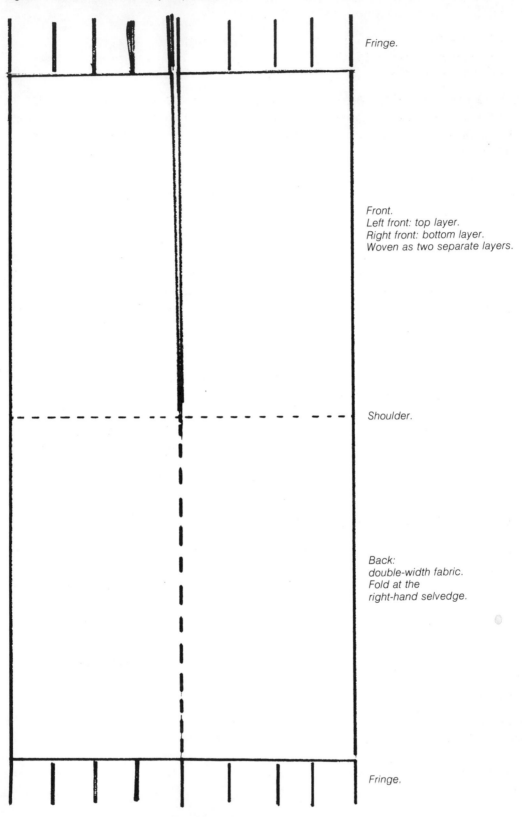

*Fringe.*

*Front.*
*Left front: top layer.*
*Right front: bottom layer.*
*Woven as two separate layers.*

*Shoulder.*

*Back:*
*double-width fabric.*
*Fold at the*
*right-hand selvedge.*

*Fringe.*

Raise harness 3. Weave one shot from right to left on the top layer.

Use one shuttle at a time and weave as follows: Leave 6 in (15.2 cm) or more of warp unwoven to use as a fringe. Starting at the left-hand selvedge, weave 1 in (2.5 cm) with weft color A, as outlined above. Weave 1 in (2.5 cm) with weft color B, as outlined above. Weave 29 in (73.7 cm) with weft color C. Should you want to increase or decrease the length of the poncho, increase or decrease the amount woven with weft color C.

*Step 2.* Weave the front of the poncho by weaving two separate layers with two shuttles, according to the treadling sequence given below:

Shuttle A. Raise harness 1. Weave one shot.
Shuttle A. Raise harness 3. Weave one shot.
Shuttle B. Raise harnesses 1 and 3 plus 2. Weave one shot.
Shuttle B. Raise harnesses 1 and 3 plus 4. Weave one shot.

Be sure to keep the weft threads separate at the selvedges to keep the two woven layers separate.

To do the weaving, use two shuttles, one for the top layer and one for the bottom layer: With two shuttles, each with weft color C, weave two separate layers for 29 in (73.7 cm). Make any necessary adjustments in the length of the poncho in this step. With two shuttles, each with weft color B, weave 1 in (2.5 cm). With two shuttles, each with weft color A, weave 1 in (2.5 cm). Leave 6 in (5.2 cm) or more of warp unwoven to use as fringe.

With Step 2, the weaving for this poncho is completed. Before starting the weaving for the bog shirt, weave 1 in (2.5 cm) in a different color as a separating strip.

To finish the poncho, when the fabric comes off the loom and the separating strip is trimmed away, the poncho is really finished. You should block and steam press it, especially to minimize the fold in the back. The fringe can be knotted or braided, if you wish.

## TO WEAVE THE BOG SHIRT

The bog shirt, so-called because it is styled on a garment unearthed in the Danish peat bogs, is usually woven in a single layer on a warp 36 in (91 cm) wide. Weavers who have looms with at least 18 in (45.7 cm) of weaving width can produce the bog shirt by using double-weave techniques.

The directions here are for a shirt with narrow bands of colors A and B at the ends of the sleeves and a wider band of colors A and B down the center of the front and back. The rest of the shirt is made up of color C (see Figure 6). To see how the shirt will look when finished, trace the diagram on a piece of paper; cut the slits and the neck opening. Then fold at the shoulders and the sides (see Figure 8).

*Step 1.* The first 13 in (33 cm) are woven with two shuttles to make two separate layers, as follows:

Shuttle A. Raise harness 1. Weave one shot.
Shuttle A. Raise harness 3. Weave one shot.

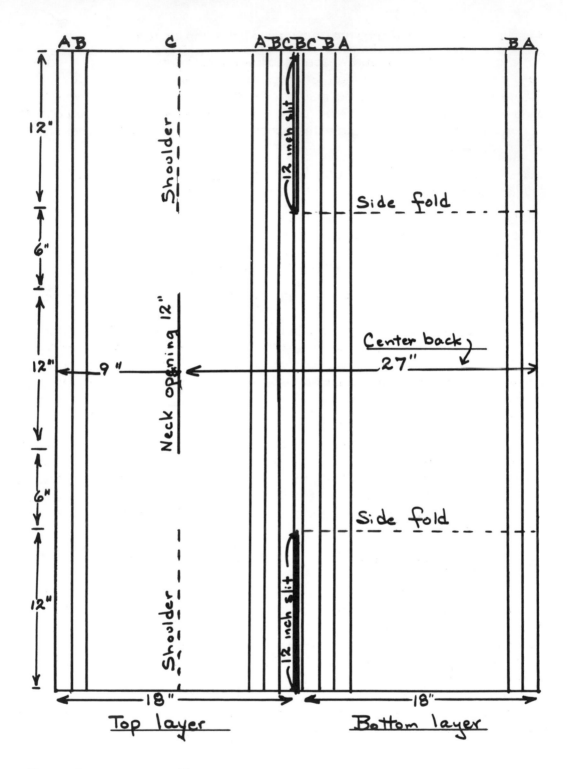

Figure 8. *Diagram of the bog shirt.*

Shuttle B. Raise harnesses 1 and 3 plus 2. Weave one shot.
Shuttle B. Raise harnesses 1 and 3 plus 4. Weave one shot.

Be sure to keep the weft threads separate at the selvedges to keep the two woven layers separate.
   The color sequence for this step is as follows:

Color A. Weave 2 in (5.1 cm).
Color B. Weave 1 in (2.5 cm).
Color C. Weave 10 in (25.4 cm).

*Step 2.* The next 6 in (15.2 cm) will be woven with one shuttle to make double-width fabric, with the fold at the right-hand selvedge. The treadling sequence is given below:

Raise harness 1. Weave one shot from left to right on the top layer.
Raise harnesses 1 and 3 plus 2. Weave one shot from right to left on the bottom layer.
Raise harnesses 1 and 3 plus 4. Weave one shot from left to right on the bottom layer.
Raise harness 3. Weave one shot from right to left on the top layer.

Weave these 6 in (15.2 cm) with color C, starting with the shuttle at the left-hand selvedge.

*Step 3.* Weave the next 12 in (30.5 cm) with two shuttles, one across half the upper layer from the left-hand selvedge to the middle, and the other across the other half of the upper layer and across the bottom layer, with the fold continuing at the right-hand selvedge. The treadling sequence is given below:

Raise harness 1. With Shuttle A, starting at the left-hand selvedge, weave one shot to the middle of the raised warp threads, across 9 in (22.9 cm) of warp. With Shuttle B, weave one shot from the middle of the raised warp threads across the other 9 in (22.9 cm) of warp to the right-hand selvedge.
Raise harnesses 1 and 3 plus 2. With Shuttle B, weave one shot from right to left across the bottom warp.
Raise harnesses 1 and 3 plus 4. With Shuttle B, weave one shot from left to right across the bottom warp.
Raise harness 3. With Shuttle B, weave one shot from the right to the middle, across 9 in (22.9 cm) of warp. With Shuttle A, weave one shot from the middle to the left-hand selvedge, across the other 9 in (22.9 cm) of warp.

In this step, the slit that is created will be the neck opening for the shirt.
   The color sequence for the 12 in (30.5 cm) is as follows:

Color C. Weave 4 in (10.2 cm).
Color B. Weave 1 in (2.5 cm).
Color A. Weave 2 in (5.1 cm).
Color B. Weave 1 in (2.5 cm).
Color C. Weave 4 in (10.2 cm).

*Step 4.* This step is a repeat of Step 2, where double-width fabric is woven with color C for 6 in (15.2 cm).

*Step 5.* This step is a repeat of the treadling sequence of Step 1, with two separate layers woven for 13 in (33 cm). The color sequence for the weaving is the reverse of Step 1, as follows:

Color C. Weave 10 in (25.4 cm).
Color B. Weave 1 in (2.5 cm).
Color A. Weave 2 in (5.1 cm).

Step 5 completes the weaving for the bog shirt.

To finish the bog shirt, block and steam press the fabric after it comes off the loom. Fold the material so that the neck opening is at the top and the two sides of the sleeves come together. Fold the two sides of the front to meet at the center front. The center stripes should match those below the neck opening. Fold under 1 in (2.5 cm) of the color A stripe of each side to form the hem running up the center front. Sew this center seam and sew the seams of the sleeves. Next sew the fabric across the bodice where the two sections come together (see Figure 9). Turn under 1 in (2.5 cm) of the color A stripe at the ends of the sleeves to make a hem for the bottom of the sleeves. When the sewing is completed, the bog shirt is finished and ready to be worn.

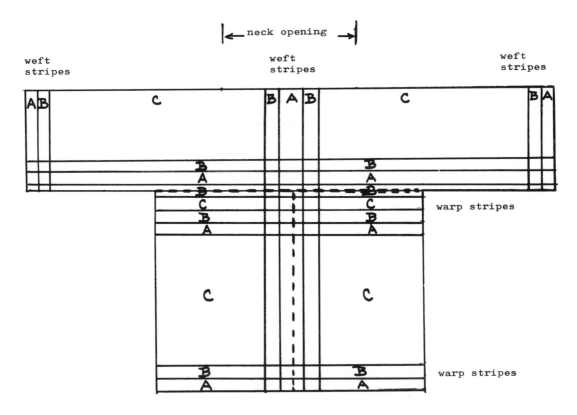

Figure 9. *Finishing the bog shirt. Sew at the dotted lines down the center front and across the bodice.*

# PART TWO

# QUILTED CLOTH, PADDED CLOTH, DOUBLE-FACED CLOTH AND REVERSIBLE PLAID CLOTH

The exercises in this section show you how to quilt or stitch two layers of cloth together, how to plan designs for stitching, and also, how to pad a design motif to give a sculptured or trapunto effect. You'll also find directions in the exercises for producing double-faced cloth, where the two layers are interlocked with a similar or dissimilar appearance, whichever you desire. In the last group of exercises in this part, you'll find instructions for several reversible plaid designs based on the two-block design concept.

To do the exercises in Part Two, prepare a warp 2 yd (1.8 m) long, following the directions as they are given in Part One. Again, the yarn should be a smooth, strong yarn in two colors, with strong contrast. Thread the loom with color A on harnesses 1 and 3, and color B on harnesses 2 and 4. Specific directions will be given for rethreading the loom for doing the reversible plaid designs, when you finish the other exercises in this section.

For weavers who made a 6-yd (5.5-m) warp for doing all the exercises in this book, I recommend that you cut off the work completed for Part One and retie the warp to the cloth beam before starting the exercises for Part Two.

Before starting the first exercise in this section, weave ½ in (1.3 cm), alternately raising harnesses 1 and 2 for one shot and harnesses 3 and 4 for the second shot, ending with both shuttles at the right-hand selvedge.

## EXERCISE 13:
# How to Quilt Two Layers of Fabric Together

A quilted fabric may be woven by using a pick-up stick to pick up from the lower layer (color B on our warp) those threads which are used to stitch or quilt the layers together. The pick-up stick should be several inches (or centimeters) longer than the warp is wide and should be smooth with a pointed end. In this first exercise for quilting, you'll get directions for picking up the tenth threads in from either side for the first quilted row and then adding more threads for the successive rows of quilting. Wind one shuttle with weft color A and one shuttle with weft color B.

*Step 1.* Weave separate layers for 1 in (2.5 cm), using the four steps of Exercise 1 as follows:

Raise harness 1. Weave one shot with color A weft.
Raise harness 3. Weave one shot with color A weft.
Raise harnesses 1 and 3 plus 2. Weave one shot with color B weft.
Raise harnesses 1 and 3 plus 4. Weave one shot with color B weft.

*Step 2.* Raise harness 2, color B warp threads. Using a pick-up stick, pick up the 10th warp thread from each end of the color B warp. Lower harness 2 and push the stick back against the reed in the beater. The two color B warp threads remain on top of the pick-up stick

Step 3. Raise harness 1 (color A) and weave one shot of color A weft. Remove the pick-up stick from the shed and beat. Lower harness 1. The weft shot passed under the raised color A warp threads and the two color B threads that were picked up.

Step 4. Raise harness 3. Weave one shot of color A weft.

Step 5. Raise harnesses 1 and 3 plus 2. Weave one shot of color B weft.

Step 6. Raise harnesses 1 and 3 plus 4. Weave one shot of color B weft.

Step 7. Weave two separate layers for 1 in (2.5 cm), using the procedure as outlined in Step 1.

Step 8. Raise harness 2, color B warp threads. Using the pick-up stick, pick up the 10th and 20th warp thread from each side. Lower harness 2 and push the pick-up stick back against the reed in the beater.

Step 9. Repeat Steps 3 through 7.

Step 10. Raise harness 2, color B warp threads. Using the pick-up stick, pick up the 10th, the 20th, and the 30th warp thread in from each side. Lower harness 2 and push the pick-up stick back against the reed in the beater.

Step 11. Repeat Steps 3 through 7.

The pattern is developed so that every 10th thread in from each side has been picked up as a stitching thread, locking the two layers together. Here, harness 2 has been used for the quilting threads, but harness 4 could have been used, or harnesses 2 and 4 could have been used together or alternately.

# EXERCISE 14:
# How to Plan a Design for Quilting Fabrics Together

Quilted fabrics may be used not only for comforters and bed coverings, but also for jackets, vests, skirts, and muffs. If you want to plan a specific design, such as initials on a bed covering, use graph paper to plot out the design and to locate it properly on the fabric. In this exercise, I've plotted out a design made of my initials and centered them on this sampler warp. While you may not care to do these same initials, if you read through the procedure carefully, you'll see how to create a design of your own. As an aid, use the full-page graph (Figure 10) as a guide in plotting the designs.

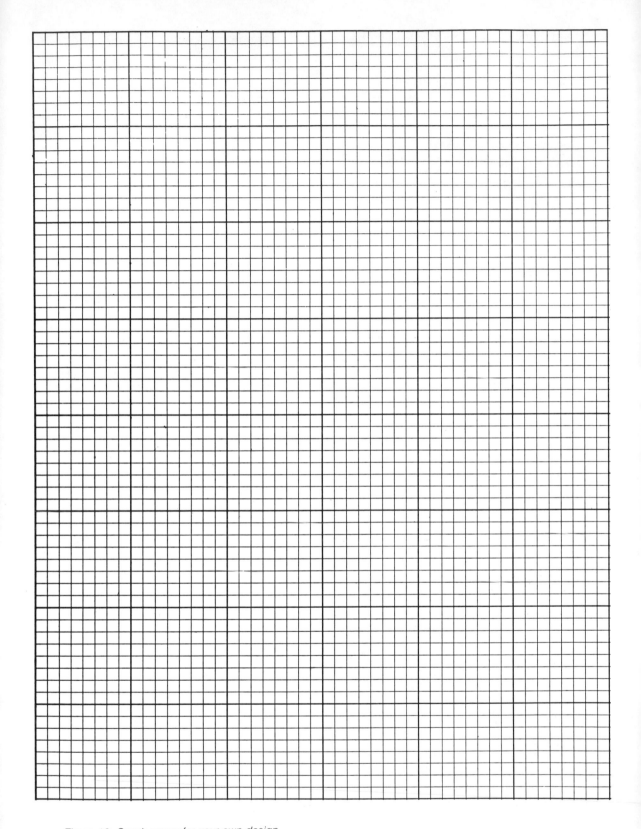

Figure 10. *Graph paper for your own design.*

Now place a sheet of tracing paper over the graph. With the tracing paper covering the graph, mark the midpoint on the bottom of the tracing paper.

Each small square on the graph can represent one, two, or more ends of the warp. For this design, I've chosen to have each square represent one warp thread. The warp ends to be picked up for creating my initials are on harness 2; with 120 ends of warp for each layer, there are 60 ends on harness 2. Because 60 ends gives an even rather than an odd number of ends, both center warp ends 30 and 31 are equidistant from the selvedges. Let's consider the middle warp thread to be the 30th warp end in from the right-hand selvedge. Count 30 squares from the + at midpoint back toward the right, each square representing one warp thread. Draw a line lengthwise at this point to mark the right-hand selvedge. Count 30 squares from the midpoint toward the left and draw a line lengthwise to mark the left-hand selvedge.

My initials are *P M W* . I've decided to have *W* as the most prominent initial, with *P* next, and *M* as the least important: therefore *W* will be the largest, with the other two initials reduced according to importance. The center of the *W* is located in the middle of the width of the warp at the 30th warp end. The *W* is now sketched on the tracing paper, starting at the third warp end from the right and ending at the 58th warp end (see Figure 11). Next, sketch in *P*, again centering it on the 30th warp end, beginning at the 16th thread and ending at the 44th thread (see Figure 11). Last of all, draw in the *M* within the confines of both the *W* and the *P,* centering on the 30th warp end extending from the 20th to the 40th warp end.

In using initials, you needn't center them all for the design to be pleasing; however, this particular design seemed to lend itself to a symmetrical approach. What is important in laying out designs, however, is for you to be aware of the center of your warp; then you can locate the design where you want it to be on the warp.

With these three initials drawn in, we can now determine which warp ends are to be picked up for outlining the letters. The pick-up rows will be spaced ½ in (1.3 cm) apart for the length of the design. The weaving is a balanced 50/50 weave, with as many weft shots to the inch (2.5 cm) as there are warp threads to the inch. At 15 ends per inch and 15 weft shots per inch (2.5 cm), we can consider eight weft shots for each half inch (1.3 cm), and for ease in weaving make every eighth row the pick-up row for the design.

Every half inch (1.3 cm) up the tracing paper design, make a short line where the outline of the initials occurs. Draw a short vertical line every ½ in (1.3 cm) along the horizontal lines of the design, as on the two lines of the upper part of the *P*. The places where the short lines are drawn indicate which warp threads will be picked up (see Figure 11). For example, in the first pick-up row at the bottom to start the base of the *W,* pick up warp ends 20 and 40. In the second pick-up row, after ½ in (1.3 cm) of weaving, pick up warp ends 18, 22, 38, and 42.

If you want to weave this design as practice, follow the directions below. If you want to make your own design, plot the outline using the tracing paper and the graph paper. Then substitute your own numbers for the warp threads to be picked up to give you the design you've outlined. In either case, the procedure for weaving will be the same.

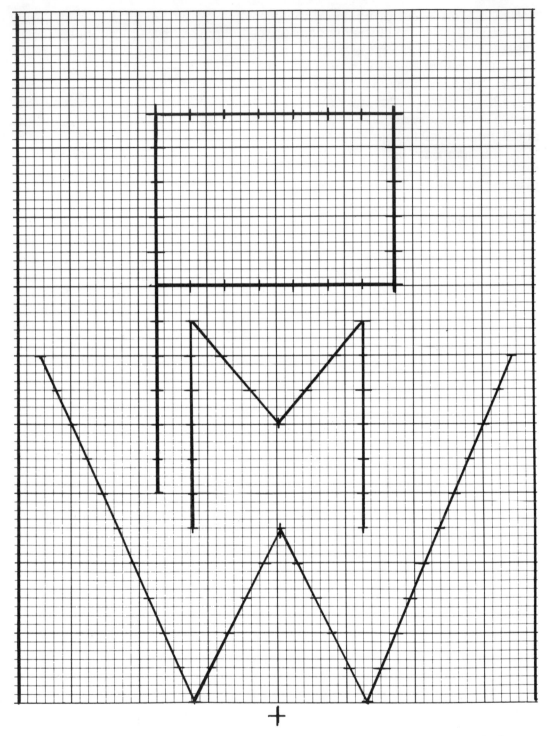

**Figure 11.** *Designing the initials PMW on graph paper. The small cross at the base of the graph marks the center of the design.*

## TO WEAVE THE DESIGN OUTLINED ON THE GRAPH

*Step 1.* Weave 1 in (2.5 cm) in two separate layers, using two shuttles.

Raise harness 1. Weave one shot of color A weft.
Raise harness 3. Weave one shot of color A weft.
Raise harnesses 1 and 3 plus 2. Weave one shot of color B weft.
Raise harnesses 1 and 3 plus 4. Weave one shot of color B weft.

*Step 2.* Weave a pick-up row by raising harness 2 and picking up the ends indicated for the first pick-up row in the list below; lower harness 2. Raise harness 1 and weave one shot of color A weft. Remove pick-up stick and beat.

*Step 3.* Complete this sequence for the two separate layers.

Raise harness 3. Weave one shot of color A weft.
Raise harnesses 1 and 3 plus 2. Weave one shot of color B weft.
Raise harnesses 1 and 3 plus 4. Weave one shot of color B weft.

*Step 4.* Weave 6 more rows on each layer, keeping the layers separate. To do this, repeat the treadling sequence of Step 1 three times.

Repeat Steps 2 through 4 until you've completed all the pick-up rows required for the design as listed below or for your own design. Then repeat Step 1 to weave 1 in (2.5 cm) above the top of the design.

The pick-up rows for the design P M W are as follows:

| Pick-Up Row | Threads to be Picked Up from Harness 2 |
|:-:|:--|
| 1 | 20, 40 |
| 2 | 18, 22, 38, 42 |
| 3 | 17, 24, 36, 44 |
| 4 | 15, 26, 34, 46 |
| 5 | 13, 28, 32, 48 |
| 6 | 12, 20, 30, 40, 49 |
| 7 | 10, 20, 40, 44, 51 |
| 8 | 8, 20, 40, 53 |
| 9 | 6, 20, 30, 40, 44, 54 |
| 10 | 5, 20, 27, 33, 40, 44, 56 |
| 11 | 3, 20, 24, 37, 40, 44, 58 |
| 12 | 20, 40, 44 |
| 13 | 16, 20, 24, 28, 32, 36, 40, 44 |
| 14 | 16, 44 |
| 15 | 16, 44 |
| 16 | 16, 44 |
| 17 | 16, 44 |
| 18 | 16, 20, 24, 28, 32, 36, 40, 44 |

*Note:* Occasionally the line indicating a pick-up warp thread seems to cross at a point where it could be one of two adjacent warp threads. In such a case, let your eyes be the guide as to which thread carries the outline of your design more smoothly.

Before starting the next exercise, weave ½ in (1.3 cm), alternately raising harnesses 1 and 2 for one shot and harnesses 3 and 4 for the second shot.

## EXERCISE 15:

# How to Achieve a Sculptured Effect on a Quilted Design

Designs can be worked out that lend themselves to padding as well as quilting to give an embossed or sculptural effect. The padding must be placed in a very thin layer; otherwise the fabric will be distorted too much. The padding should be inserted as the weaving progresses, preferably after completing the sequence for each quilting row.

Two designs will be detailed for you, one a cross and the other a heart. If you prefer to do a different design, read through the instructions to familiarize yourself with the procedure. Then using tracing paper and the graph, draw out your own design and mark the correct threads to be picked up for each row.

### TO WEAVE AN EMBOSSED CROSS DESIGN

This design (see Figure 12) is composed of narrow vertical and horizontal areas. Since a major portion of the vertical design would utilize the same warp threads for pick-up threads for a considerable length of the design, it would be better to use both harnesses 2 and 4 for the pick-up threads. Otherwise there would be too much stress placed on several ends of the lower warp, as they are used repeatedly as pick-up threads. Because harnesses 2 and 4 are alternated for the pick-up ends, there is considerably less stress placed on individual warp threads.

The procedure for weaving and padding this design is as follows:

*Step 1.* Weave 1 in (2.5 cm) for two separate layers using the treadling below:

Raise harness 1. Weave one shot of color A weft.
Raise harness 3. Weave one shot of color A weft.
Raise harnesses 1 and 3 plus 2. Weave one shot of color B weft.
Raise harnesses 1 and 3 plus 4. Weave one shot of color B weft.

*Step 2.* Raise harness 2. Pick up the ends indicated for the first pick-up row of the design. Lower harness 2 and raise harness 1. Weave one shot of color A weft. Remove the pick-up stick and beat.

*Step 3.* Complete this sequence for the two separate layers.

Raise harness 3. Weave one shot of color A weft.
Raise harnesses 1 and 3 plus 2. Weave one shot of color B weft.

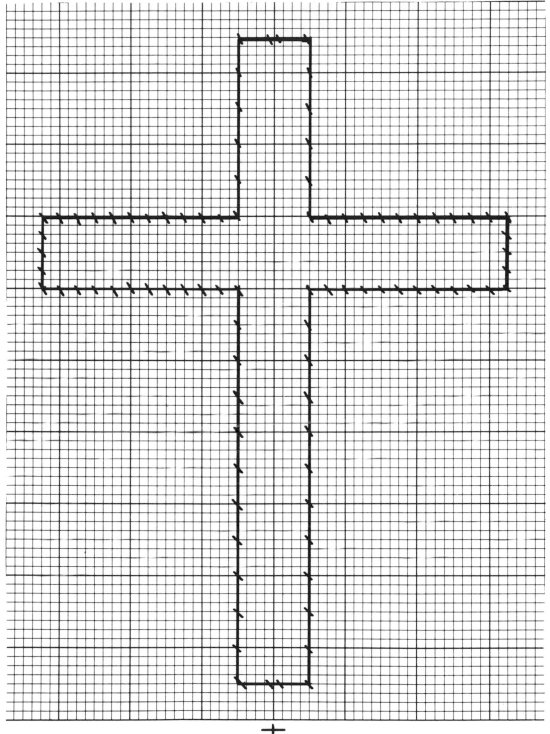

Figure 12. *Embossed cross design.*

Raise harnesses 1 and 3 plus 4. Weave one shot of color B weft.

*Step 4.* Weave six more rows on each layer; to do this, repeat the treadling sequence of Step 1 three times.

*Step 5.* Raise harness 4. Pick up the ends indicated for the second pick-up row of the design. Lower harness 4. Raise harness 1 and weave one shot of color A weft. Remove the pick-up stick and beat.

*Step 6.* Repeat the procedure for Step 3.

*Step 7.* Raise harnesses 1 and 3. Using a small amount of pillow stuffing, pad the areas between the pick-up threads (in this case, between warp ends 27 and 34). The amount of padding used should be just enough to cause the area between the two outside pick-up threads to be slightly elevated, without distortion of the areas beyond them.

*Step 8.* Repeat Step 4 in order to weave six more rows on each layer.

Repeat Steps 2 through 8 until you've woven the first 11 rows of pick-up threads for the cross design, thereby completing the lower portion of the cross.

Pick-up rows 12 through 16 on the list create the outline for the arms of the cross. The weaving procedure for this area is again a repeat of Steps 2 through 8, with the one exception being in Step 4, where only two more rows (instead of six) are woven for each layer. Thus, the pick-up rows will occur every fourth row instead of every eighth for this part of the design in order to give added importance to this area.

To weave and pad the upper vertical portion of the cross, follow the procedure in Steps 2 through 8 but now weaving six more rows for each layer again in Step 4. Pick-up rows 17 through 21 complete the weaving of the cross. Be sure to insert whatever padding is necessary before doing pick-up row 21, which closes the top of the design. Finish with a heading of 1 in (2.5 cm), woven in two separate layers, as given in Step 1.

The pick-up rows and ends for the cross design are as follows:

| Row | Ends | Harness |
|---|---|---|
| 1 | 27, 30, 31, 34 | 2 |
| 2 | 27, 34 | 4 |
| 3 | 27, 34 | 2 |
| 4 | 27, 34 | 4 |
| 5 | 27, 34 | 2 |
| 6 | 27, 34 | 4 |
| 7 | 27, 34 | 2 |
| 8 | 27, 34 | 4 |
| 9 | 27, 34 | 2 |
| 10 | 27, 34 | 4 |
| 11 | 27, 34 | 2 |
| 12 | 5, 7, 9, 11, 13, 15, 17, 19, 21, 23, 25, 27, 34, 36, 38, 40, 42, 44, 46, 48, 50, 52, 54, 56 | 4 |

| 13 | 5, 56 | 2 |
| 14 | 5, 56 | 4 |
| 15 | 5, 56 | 2 |
| 16 | 5, 7, 9, 11, 13, 15, 17, 19, 21, 23, 25, 27, 34, 36, 38, 40, 42, 44, 46, 48, 50, 52, 54, 56 | 4 |
| 17 | 27, 34 | 2 |
| 18 | 27, 34 | 4 |
| 19 | 27, 34 | 2 |
| 20 | 27, 34 | 4 |
| 21 | 27, 30, 31, 34 | 2 |

## TO WEAVE AN EMBOSSED HEART DESIGN

The heart design (see Figure 13) is made up of curves and slanting lines rather than the straight horizontal and vertical lines of the cross design. If the pick-up

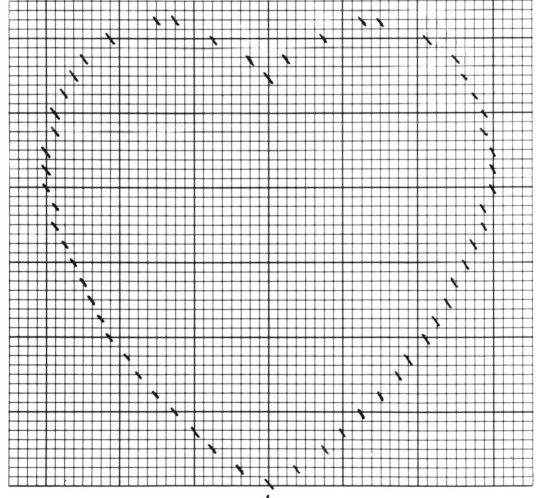

Figure 13. *Embossed heart design.*

rows occur every fourth row instead of every eighth row, the shape will be more clearly defined.

The procedure for weaving and padding the heart design is as follows:

*Step 1.* Weave 1 in (2.5 cm) for two separate layers, using the treadling below:

Raise harness 1. Weave one shot of color A weft.
Raise harness 3. Weave one shot of color A weft.
Raise harnesses 1 and 3 plus 2. Weave one shot of color B weft.
Raise harnesses 1 and 3 plus 4. Weave one shot of color B weft.

*Step 2.* Raise harness 2. Pick up the ends indicated for the first pick-up row on the list given at the end of these instructions. Lower harness 2 and raise harness 1. Weave one shot of color A weft. Remove the pick-up stick and beat.

*Step 3.* Complete this sequence for two separate layers:

Raise harness 3. Weave one shot of color A weft.
Raise harnesses 1 and 3 plus 2. Weave one shot of color B weft.
Raise harnesses 1 and 3 plus 4. Weave one shot of color B weft.

*Step 4.* Weave two more rows on each layer. To do this, repeat the treadling sequence of Step 1 just once.

The complete heart design is woven by repeating Steps 2 through 4 until you finish all the pick-up rows on the list as given. The padding should be put in place as the weaving progresses. After every second pick-up row, raise harnesses 1 and 3; place a small amount of padding, such as pillow stuffing or unspun fleece, in the area between the pick-up threads. The amount of padding should be just enough to cause the design area to be slightly elevated without distortion to the area beyond. Before you weave pick-up row 26, be sure that the necessary padding is in place, as row 26 closes the top of the heart design. Finish with a heading of 1 in (2.5 cm), woven in two separate layers, as given in Step 1.

The pick-up rows and ends for the heart design are given as follows:

| Row | Ends on Harness 2 |
|---|---|
| 1 | 32 |
| 2 | 29, 35 |
| 3 | 26, 38 |
| 4 | 24, 40 |
| 5 | 22, 42 |
| 6 | 20, 44 |
| 7 | 18, 46 |
| 8 | 17, 47 |
| 9 | 15, 49 |
| 10 | 14, 50 |
| 11 | 13, 51 |
| 12 | 12, 52 |
| 13 | 11, 53 |
| 14 | 10, 54 |
| 15 | 9, 55 |

| 16 | 9, 55 |
|----|-------|
| 17 | 8, 56 |
| 18 | 8, 56 |
| 19 | 8, 56 |
| 20 | 9, 55 |
| 21 | 9, 55 |
| 22 | 10, 54 |
| 23 | 11, 32, 53 |
| 24 | 12, 30, 34, 52 |
| 25 | 15, 26, 38, 49 |
| 26 | 20, 22, 42, 44 |

Before starting the next exercise, weave for ½ in (1.3 cm), alternately raising harnesses 1 and 2 for one shot and harnesses 3 and 4 for the second shot.

# EXERCISE 16:
# How to Weave Double-Faced Fabric

One use of double weave is the production of a double-faced fabric in which the two layers are interlocked, with a twill-weave appearance on both sides. The treadling is a sequence of eight steps, with one shot in warp-faced twill for one layer alternating with one shot in weft-faced twill for the other layer. The interlocking of the two layers produces a single-layered, reinforced fabric suitable for blankets, draperies, upholstery, suiting, and rugs.

The warp on which we are weaving these exercises has color A on harnesses 1 and 3 with color B on harnesses 2 and 4. As the two twill sequences are woven, the two colors will show mixed on both sides of the fabric; one side will be predominantly color A and the other will be predominantly color B.

In the first part of this exercise, you'll use color A for the weft on the top layer and color B for the weft for the bottom layer. The treadling sequence is as follows:

*Step 1.* Raise harness 1. Weave one shot of color A.

*Step 2.* Raise harnesses 1–2–3. Weave one shot of color B.

*Step 3.* Raise harness 2. Weave one shot of color A.

*Step 4.* Raise harnesses 2–3–4. Weave one shot of color B.

*Step 5.* Raise harness 3. Weave one shot of color A.

*Step 6.* Raise harnesses 3–4–1. Weave one shot of color B.

*Step 7.* Raise harness 4. Weave one shot of color A.

*Step 8.* Raise harnesses 4–1–2. Weave one shot of color B.

Repeat Steps 1 through 8 for 3 in (7.6 cm). Notice how the upper side of the fabric differs from the opposite side. Before starting the next part of this exercise, weave ½ in (1.3 cm), alternately raising harnesses 1 and 2 for one shot and harnesses 3 and 4 for the second shot.

In the second part of this exercise, you'll use color B for the top layer and color A for the bottom layer. The treadling sequence is as follows:

*Step 1.* Raise harness 1. Weave one shot of color B.

*Step 2.* Raise harnesses 1–2–3. Weave one shot of color A.

*Step 3.* Raise harness 2. Weave one shot of color B.

*Step 4.* Raise harnesses 2–3–4. Weave one shot of color A.

*Step 5.* Raise harness 3. Weave one shot of color B.

*Step 6.* Raise harnesses 3–4–1. Weave one shot of color A.

*Step 7.* Raise harness 4. Weave one shot of color B.

*Step 8.* Raise harnesses 4–1–2. Weave one shot of color A.

Repeat Steps 1 through 8 for 3 in (7.6 cm). Again, notice how the upper side differs from the lower side and what a firm interlocked fabric has been produced.

A warp specifically designed to weave double-faced fabric could be all one color; if the warp color is then used for the weft in one twill sequence and a different weft is used for the other twill sequence, the resulting fabric would be all one color on one side and mixed colors on the other. Such a fabric would be ideally suited for reversible clothing. One weft could be a textured yarn, such as a bouclé or a flake mohair for the upper side, reinforced by the use of a strong worsted yarn for the underside. If fabric for clothing interests you, make a small separate warp and try out some combinations of wefts using the same eight-step treadling sequence.

In the projects that follow the exercises in Part Two, there will be a discussion of double-faced rugs, with directions given for planning and weaving one. Before starting the next exercise, weave ½ in (1.3 cm), alternately raising harnesses 1 and 2 for one shot and harnesses 3 and 4 for the second shot.

# EXERCISE 17:
# How to Weave Reversible Plaid Designs in Double Weave

The exercises woven up to this point have utilized a solid color A warp for one layer, with a solid color B warp for the other layer. The series of plaid designs for Exercise 17 will have stripes of color A and color B on each layer of the double-weave warp. The one layer will be threaded on harnesses 1 and 3 and the other layer will be threaded on harnesses 2 and 4, just as we've done earlier.

It won't be necessary to make a new warp, as specific directions for rethreading the loom will be given for each design. The designs are based on the two-block design concept; where a stripe of color A appears on the top layer of warp, there'll be a corresponding stripe of color B on the bottom layer. In the same way, where a stripe of color B appears on the top layer, a corresponding stripe of color A will be on the bottom layer.

In weaving the designs, color A weft for the top layer (harnesses 1 and 3) produces areas of solid color A warp and weft, and areas of mixed warp color B and weft color A. Color B weft on the bottom layer (harnesses 2 and 4) gives solid areas of color B, and areas of mixed warp A and weft B. If the layers are then reversed, with harnesses 2 and 4 as the top layer, weaving with weft color A produces solid blocks of color A warp and weft where the mixed areas were, as well as mixed color areas where solid color A previously appeared on the top layer. Since harnesses 1 and 3 have become the bottom layer in this reversal, color B weft for the bottom would move the solid B areas to those previously of mixed color, and vice versa. In the directions for weaving and in the diagrams of each design, you'll see how this interchange of layers can be used to produce interesting patterns for weaving blankets, throws, table runners, and even "op art" pillows.

## PREPARING THE LOOM FOR RETHREADING

With Exercises 13 through 16 still on the loom, move the warp forward until you have about 6 in (15.2 cm) of unwoven warp in front of the harnesses. Raise harnesses 1 and 3 and place a lease stick in the shed created *behind* the harnesses. Raise harnesses 2 and 4 and place a second lease stick in the second shed created *behind* the harnesses. Secure the lease sticks firmly together at each end. You have now established a threading cross on the lease sticks behind the harnesses.

Now cut approximately 30 or 32 warp threads (about 1 in or 2.5 cm of the width of the warp) in *front* of the harnesses, about 3 in (7.6 cm) above the ½-in (1.3-cm)

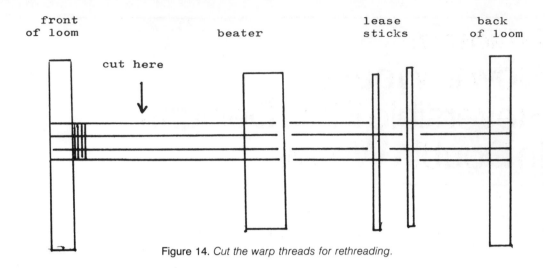

front
of loom

beater

lease
sticks

back
of loom

cut here

Figure 14. *Cut the warp threads for rethreading.*

strip woven at the end of Exercise 16 (see Figure 14). Pull these warp ends out of the heddles and let them hang behind the harnesses in front of the lease sticks. You may want to knot together each inch (2.5 cm) group of warp ends to keep them from slipping out of the lease sticks until you have all the warp threads ready for rethreading. Continue across the width of the warp, each time cutting about 30 or 32 warp threads at a point 3 in (7.6 cm) above the end of the weaving and pulling them out of the heddles to the back of the harnesses.

Once you have all the warp threads cut and secured behind the harnesses with the threading order held intact by the lease sticks, remove the weaving produced for Exercises 13 through 16. The loom is now ready for rethreading for any one of the three plaid designs that follow. Each design is given for 120 threads per layer at 15 ends per inch (2.5 cm) and for 128 threads per layer at 16 ends per inch.

## TO WEAVE PLAID DESIGN NO. 1

This first design is a series of warp stripes, narrow at each selvedge, and increasing gradually, with the center stripe the widest. The diagram for threading the warp at 120 ends per layer is given in Figure 15; the diagram for threading the warp at 128 ends per layer is given in Figure 16.

As an aid to help you interpret these diagrams, notice that the first group of warps on each layer is made up of four threads; for one layer there are four warp ends of color A, while on the other layer there are four ends of color B. Take the first eight warp ends on the lease sticks behind the heddles; you'll find that there are four ends of color A alternating with four ends of color B. Thread the first end of color A on harness 1; thread the first end of color B on harness 2. Thread the second end of color A on harness 3; thread the second end of color B on harness 4. Repeat this sequence to thread the first eight ends with color A on harnesses 1 and 3, while color B ends are threaded on harnesses 2 and 4.

The second group of warps for each layer is also made up of eight ends, four ends of color B for harnesses 1 and 3, with four ends of color A for harnesses 2 and 4. Take the next eight ends of warp. Thread the first end of color B on harness 1; thread the first end of color A on harness 2. Thread the second end of color B

*One layer on harnesses 1 and 3.*

| 4 | 4 | 4 | 8 | 8 | 12 | 12 | 16 | 12 | 12 | 8 | 8 | 4 | 4 | 4 |
|---|---|---|---|---|----|----|----|----|----|---|---|---|---|---|
| A | B | A | B | A | B | A | B | A | B | A | B | A | B | A |

*The second layer on harnesses 2 and 4.*

| 4 | 4 | 4 | 8 | 8 | 12 | 12 | 16 | 12 | 12 | 8 | 8 | 4 | 4 | 4 |
|---|---|---|---|---|----|----|----|----|----|---|---|---|---|---|
| B | A | B | A | B | A | B | A | B | A | B | A | B | A | B |

Figure 15. *Plaid Design No. 1. 120 threads per layer.*

*One layer on harnesses 1 and 3.*

| 4 | 4 | 4 | 4 | 8 | 8 | 12 | 12 | 16 | 12 | 12 | 8 | 8 | 4 | 4 | 4 | 4 |
|---|---|---|---|---|---|----|----|----|----|----|---|---|---|---|---|---|
| A | B | A | B | A | B | A | B | A | B | A | B | A | B | A | B | A |

*The second layer on harnesses 2 and 4.*

| 4 | 4 | 4 | 4 | 8 | 8 | 12 | 12 | 16 | 12 | 12 | 8 | 8 | 4 | 4 | 4 | 4 |
|---|---|---|---|---|---|----|----|----|----|----|---|---|---|---|---|---|
| B | A | B | A | B | A | B | A | B | A | B | A | B | A | B | A | B |

Figure 16. *Plaid Design No. 1. 128 threads per layer.*

on harness 3; thread the second end of color A on harness 4. Repeat this sequence in order to thread the second eight warp threads with color B on harnesses 1 and 3, while color A warps are on harnesses 2 and 4.

Follow this same procedure across the row for the threading. If there are four ends of color A on harnesses 1 and 3, there will be four ends of color B on harnesses 2 and 4. Take the next eight ends in the order established by the threading cross on the lease sticks; the color A ends will be threaded with the first one on harness 1 followed by the first color B on harness 2; the second color A will be on harness 3, and the second color B will be on harness 4. In the same way, if there are eight ends of color B on harnesses 1 and 3, there will be eight ends of color A on harnesses 2 and 4. To thread them, take the next 16 warp ends from the lease sticks and place the color B ends alternately on harnesses 1 and 3 with the ends of color A on harnesses 2 and 4, at all times maintaining the threading order 1–2–3–4. The end result of this threading will give warp stripes of color A and color B alternating across each layer of the warp. After you've finished threading and resleying the warp, lash the warp to the cloth beam and you're ready to weave Plaid Design No. 1.

The diagram for weaving this plaid shows weft blocks that increase in height in the same proportion as the warp stripes increase in width (see Figure 17 for 120 ends per layer and Figure 18 for 128 ends per layer). Each small square on the diagram represents four warp threads in width and four weft shots in height for each layer. Thus for the warps with 128 ends per layer, there is an additional square at each side of the design and an additional square at the top and at the bottom.

Two treadling sequences are used. One considers harnesses 1 and 3 to be the top layer, and the other uses harnesses 2 and 4 as the top layer. The first treadling sequence is as follows:

*Step 1.* Raise harness 1. Weave one shot of color A.

*Step 2.* Raise harness 3. Weave one shot of color A.

*Step 3.* Raise harnesses 1 and 3 plus 2. Weave one shot of color B.

*Step 4.* Raise harnesses 1 and 3 plus 4. Weave one shot of color B.

The second treadling sequence is as follows:

*Step 1.* Raise harness 2. Weave one shot of color A.

*Step 2.* Raise harness 4. Weave one shot of color A.

*Step 3.* Raise harnesses 2 and 4 plus 1. Weave one shot of color B.

*Step 4.* Raise harnesses 2 and 4 plus 3. Weave one shot of color B weft.

Each treadling sequence weaves two rows on each layer. Repeating the sequence once produces four rows on each layer, which are the four weft shots represented by each square in the height of the diagram. To weave Plaid Design No. 1, follow the order of the treadling sequences as given below, weaving each sequence the number of times specified on the list.

For 120 ends per layer of warp:

| Step | Treadling Sequence | Number of Times |
|------|--------------------|-----------------|
| 1 | No. 1 | 2 |
| 2 | No. 2 | 2 |
| 3 | No. 1 | 2 |
| 4 | No. 2 | 4 |
| 5 | No. 1 | 4 |
| 6 | No. 2 | 6 |
| 7 | No. 1 | 6 |
| 8 | No. 2 | 8 |
| 9 | No. 1 | 6 |
| 10 | No. 2 | 6 |
| 11 | No. 1 | 4 |
| 12 | No. 2 | 4 |
| 13 | No. 1 | 2 |
| 14 | No. 2 | 2 |
| 15 | No. 1 | 2 |

Figure 17. *Diagram for Plaid Design No. 1. 120 threads per layer.*

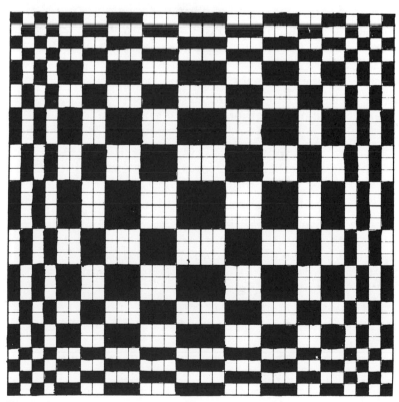

Figure 18. *Diagram for Plaid Design No. 1. 128 threads per layer.*

For 128 ends per layer of warp:

| Step | Treadling Sequence | Number of Times |
|:---:|:---:|:---:|
| 1 | No. 1 | 2 |
| 2 | No. 2 | 2 |
| 3 | No. 1 | 2 |
| 4 | No. 2 | 2 |
| 5 | No. 1 | 4 |
| 6 | No. 2 | 4 |
| 7 | No. 1 | 6 |
| 8 | No. 2 | 6 |
| 9 | No. 1 | 8 |
| 10 | No. 2 | 6 |
| 11 | No. 1 | 6 |
| 12 | No. 2 | 4 |
| 13 | No. 1 | 4 |
| 14 | No. 2 | 2 |
| 15 | No. 1 | 2 |
| 16 | No. 2 | 2 |
| 17 | No. 1 | 2 |

## TO WEAVE PLAID DESIGN NO. 2

The second plaid design is a series of narrow stripes on either side of a series of wide warp stripes. The diagram for threading the warp at 120 ends per layer is given in Figure 19; the diagram for threading the warp at 128 ends per layer is given in Figure 20.

As an aid to help you interpret the diagrams, notice that the first group of warps on each layer is made up of four threads; for one layer there are four warp ends of color A, while on the other layer there are four ends of color B. Take the first eight warp ends on the lease sticks behind the heddles; you'll find that there are four ends of color A alternating with four ends of color B. Thread the first end of color A on harness 1; thread the first end of color B on harness 2. Thread the second end of color A on harness 3; thread the second end of color B on harness 4. Repeat this sequence and you'll find that you've threaded the first eight ends, with color A on harnesses 1 and 3, while color B ends are on harnesses 2 and 4.

The second group of warps for each layer is also made up of eight ends, four ends of color B for harnesses 1 and 3 and four ends of color A on harnesses 2 and 4. Thread the first end of color B on harness 1; then thread the first end of color A on harness 2. Thread the second end of color B on harness 3 and the second end of color A on harness 4. Repeat this sequence and you'll have threaded the second eight warps with color B on harnesses 1 and 3, while color A warps are on harnesses 2 and 4.

Follow this same procedure for all the threading. In the areas where there are 16 ends of color A for one layer, there will be 16 ends of color B for the other layer. The threading order remains the same, a straight threading, 1–2–3–4, but there'll be warp stripes of color A alternating with stripes of Color B on each layer. After

One layer harnesses 1 and 3.

| 4 | 4 | 4 | 4 | 4 | 16 | 16 | 16 | 16 | 16 | 4 | 4 | 4 | 4 | 4 |
|---|---|---|---|---|----|----|----|----|----|---|---|---|---|---|
| A | B | A | B | A | B | A | B | A | B | A | B | A | B | A |

The second layer on harnesses 2 and 4.

| 4 | 4 | 4 | 4 | 4 | 16 | 16 | 16 | 16 | 16 | 4 | 4 | 4 | 4 | 4 |
|---|---|---|---|---|----|----|----|----|----|---|---|---|---|---|
| B | A | B | A | B | A | B | A | B | A | B | A | B | A | B |

Figure 19. *Plaid Design No. 2. 120 threads per layer.*

One layer on harnesses 1 and 3.

| 4 | 4 | 4 | 4 | 4 | 4 | 16 | 16 | 16 | 16 | 16 | 4 | 4 | 4 | 4 | 4 | 4 |
|---|---|---|---|---|---|----|----|----|----|----|---|---|---|---|---|---|
| A | B | A | B | A | B | A | B | A | B | A | B | A | B | A | B | A |

The second layer on harnesses 2 and 4.

| 4 | 4 | 4 | 4 | 4 | 4 | 16 | 16 | 16 | 16 | 16 | 4 | 4 | 4 | 4 | 4 | 4 |
|---|---|---|---|---|---|----|----|----|----|----|---|---|---|---|---|---|
| B | A | B | A | B | A | B | A | B | A | B | A | B | A | B | A | B |

Figure 20. *Plaid Design No. 2. 128 threads per layer.*

you've finished threading and resleying the warp, lash the warp to the cloth beam. Now you're ready to weave Plaid Design No. 2.

The diagram for weaving Plaid Design No. 2 shows a series of narrow weft stripes at the top and at the bottom; in between is a series of wide weft stripes (see Figure 21 for the warp 120 ends per layer and Figure 22 for the warp 128 ends per layer). Each small square on the diagram represents four warp threads in width and four weft shots in height for each layer. Thus, for the warps at 128 ends per layer, there is an additional square at each side of the design and an additional square at the top and the bottom.

Two treadling sequences are used, one that uses harnesses 1 and 3 for the top layer, and one that uses harnesses 2 and 4 as the top layer. The first treadling sequence is as follows:

*Step 1.* Raise harness 1. Weave one shot of color A weft.

*Step 2.* Raise harness 3. Weave one shot of color A.

*Step 3.* Raise harnesses 1 and 3 plus 2. Weave one shot of color B.

*Step 4.* Raise harnesses 1 and 3 plus 4. Weave one shot of color B.

This is the second treadling sequence:

*Step 1.* Raise harness 2. Weave one shot of color A weft.

*Step 2.* Raise harness 4. Weave one shot of color A.

*Step 3.* Raise harnesses 2 and 4 plus 1. Weave one shot of color B.

*Step 4.* Raise harnesses 2 and 4 plus 3. Weave one shot of color B.

Each treadling sequence weaves two rows on each layer. Repeating the sequence once produces four rows on each layer which are the four weft shots represented by each square in the height of the design on the diagram. To weave Plaid Design No. 2, follow the order of the treadling sequences as given below, weaving each sequence the number of times specified on the list.

For 120 ends per layer of warp:

| Step | Treadling Sequence | Number of Times |
|------|--------------------|-----------------|
| 1 | No. 1 | 2 |
| 2 | No. 2 | 2 |
| 3 | No. 1 | 2 |
| 4 | No. 2 | 2 |
| 5 | No. 1 | 2 |
| 6 | No. 2 | 8 |
| 7 | No. 1 | 8 |
| 8 | No. 2 | 8 |
| 9 | No. 1 | 8 |
| 10 | No. 2 | 8 |
| 11 | No. 1 | 2 |
| 12 | No. 2 | 2 |
| 13 | No. 1 | 2 |
| 14 | No. 2 | 2 |
| 15 | No. 1 | 2 |

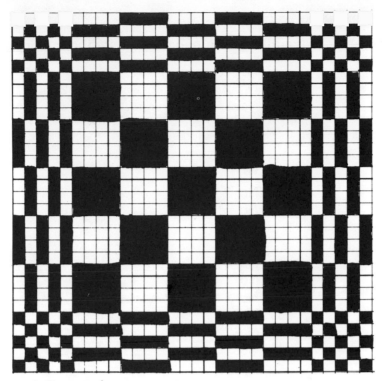

**Figure 21.** *Diagram for Plaid Design No. 2. 120 threads per layer.*

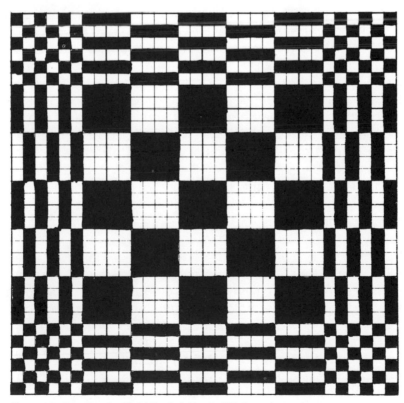

**Figure 22.** *Diagram for Plaid Design No. 2. 128 threads per layer.*

69

For 128 ends per layer of warp:

| Step | Treadling Sequence | Number of Times |
|:---:|:---:|:---:|
| 1 | No. 1 | 2 |
| 2 | No. 2 | 2 |
| 3 | No. 1 | 2 |
| 4 | No. 2 | 2 |
| 5 | No. 1 | 2 |
| 6 | No. 2 | 2 |
| 7 | No. 1 | 8 |
| 8 | No. 2 | 8 |
| 9 | No. 1 | 8 |
| 10 | No. 2 | 8 |
| 11 | No. 1 | 8 |
| 12 | No. 2 | 2 |
| 13 | No. 1 | 2 |
| 14 | No. 2 | 2 |
| 15 | No. 1 | 2 |
| 16 | No. 2 | 2 |
| 17 | No. 1 | 2 |

## TO WEAVE PLAID DESIGN NO. 3

The third plaid design has a series of wide warp stripes with one or two narrow stripes in between them. The diagram for threading the warp at 120 ends per layer is given in Figure 23; the diagram for threading the warp at 128 ends per layer is given in Figure 24.

As an aid to help you interpret the diagrams, notice that the first group of warps on each layer is made up of four threads; for one layer there are four warp ends of color A, while on the other layer there are four ends of color B. Take the first eight warp ends on the lease sticks behind the harnesses; you'll find that there are four ends of color A alternating with four ends of color B. Thread the first end of color A on harness 1; thread the first end of color B on harness 2. Thread the second end of color A on harness 3; thread the second end of color B on harness 4. Repeat this sequence to thread the first eight ends, with color A on harnesses 1 and 3 and color B ends on harnesses 2 and 4. These eight threads make up one narrow stripe in each layer.

In the wide stripes, there are 16 ends of one color on one layer with 16 ends of the other color on the other layer. The threading procedure remains the same: a straight threading of 1–2–3–4 until you have 16 ends of one color on harnesses 1 and 3, and 16 ends of the other color on harnesses 2 and 4. The end result will produce warp stripes of color A and color B alternating all across each layer of the warp. After you finish threading and resleying the warp, lash the warp to the cloth beam and you're ready to weave Plaid Design No. 3.

The diagram for weaving this plaid design shows narrow weft stripes in between wide weft stripes, following the same proportions of the stripes in the warp (see Figure 25 for 120 ends per layer and Figure 26 for 128 ends per layer). Each

*One layer on harnesses 1 and 3.*

| 4 | 16 | 4 | 4 | 16 | 4 | 4 | 16 | 4 | 4 | 16 | 4 | 4 | 16 | 4 |
|---|----|---|---|----|---|---|----|---|---|----|---|---|----|---|
| A | B | A | B | A | B | A | B | A | B | A | B | A | B | A |

*The second layer on harnesses 2 and 4.*

| 4 | 16 | 4 | 4 | 16 | 4 | 4 | 16 | 4 | 4 | 16 | 4 | 4 | 16 | 4 |
|---|----|---|---|----|---|---|----|---|---|----|---|---|----|---|
| B | A | B | A | B | A | B | A | B | A | B | A | B | A | B |

**Figure 23.** *Plaid Design No. 3. 120 threads per layer.*

*One layer on harnesses 1 and 3.*

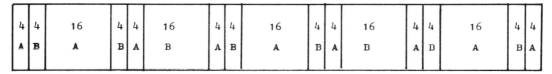

| 4 | 4 | 16 | 4 | 4 | 16 | 4 | 4 | 16 | 4 | 4 | 16 | 4 | 4 | 16 | 4 | 4 |
|---|---|----|---|---|----|---|---|----|---|---|----|---|---|----|---|---|
| A | B | A | B | A | B | A | B | A | B | A | D | A | D | A | B | A |

*The second layer on harnesses 2 and 4.*

| 4 | 4 | 16 | 4 | 4 | 16 | 4 | 4 | 16 | 4 | 4 | 16 | 4 | 4 | 16 | 4 | 4 |
|---|---|----|---|---|----|---|---|----|---|---|----|---|---|----|---|---|
| B | A | B | A | B | A | B | A | B | A | B | A | B | A | B | A | B |

**Figure 24.** *Plaid Design No. 3. 128 threads per layer.*

small square on the diagram represents four warp threads in width and four weft shots in height for each layer. Thus for the warps with 128 ends per layer, there is an additional square at each side of the design and an additional square at the top and at the bottom.

Two treadling sequences are used for the weaving, one using harnesses 1 and 3 for the top layer, the other using harnesses 2 and 4 for the top layer. The first treadling sequence follows:

*Step 1.* Raise harness 1. Weave one shot of color A weft.

*Step 2.* Raise harness 3. Weave one shot of color A weft.

*Step 3.* Raise harnesses 1 and 3 plus 2. Weave one shot of color B weft.

*Step 4.* Raise harnesses 1 and 3 plus 4. Weave one shot of color B weft.

The second treadling sequence is as follows:

*Step 1.* Raise harness 2. Weave one shot of color A weft.

*Step 2.* Raise harness 4. Weave one shot of color A weft.

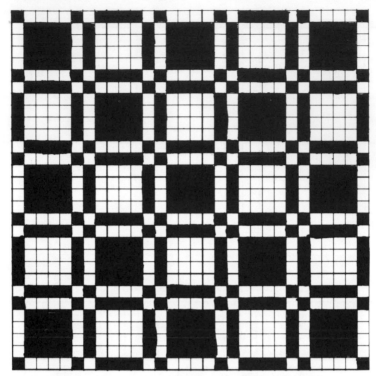

**Figure 25.** *Diagram of Plaid Design No. 3. 120 threads per layer.*

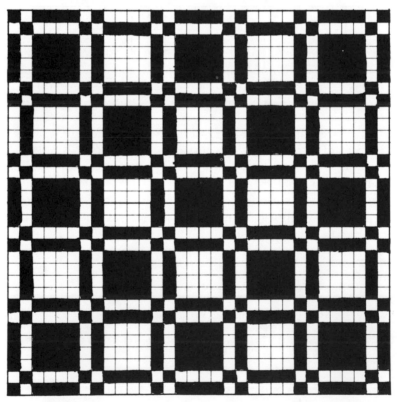

**Figure 26.** *Diagram of Plaid Design No. 3. 128 threads per layer.*

*Step 3.* Raise harnesses 2 and 4 plus 1. Weave one shot of color B weft.

*Step 4.* Raise harnesses 2 and 4 plus 3. Weave one shot of color B weft.

Each treadling sequence weaves two rows on each layer. Repeating the sequence once produces four rows on each layer which are the four weft shots represented by each square in the height of the diagram.

To weave Plaid Design No. 3, follow the order of the treadling sequences given below, weaving each sequence the number of times specified on the list. For 120 ends per layer of warp:

| Step | Treadling Sequence | Number of Times |
|------|--------------------|-----------------|
| 1 | No. 1 | 2 |
| 2 | No. 2 | 8 |
| 3 | No. 1 | 2 |
| 4 | No. 2 | 2 |
| 5 | No. 1 | 8 |
| 6 | No. 2 | 2 |
| 7 | No. 1 | 2 |
| 8 | No. 2 | 8 |
| 9 | No. 1 | 2 |
| 10 | No. 2 | 2 |
| 11 | No. 1 | 8 |
| 12 | No. 2 | 2 |
| 13 | No. 1 | 2 |
| 14 | No. 2 | 8 |
| 15 | No. 1 | 2 |

For 128 ends per layer of warp:

| Step | Treadling Sequence | Number of Times |
|------|--------------------|-----------------|
| 1 | No. 1 | 2 |
| 2 | No. 2 | 2 |
| 3 | No. 1 | 8 |
| 4 | No. 2 | 2 |
| 5 | No. 1 | 2 |
| 6 | No. 2 | 8 |
| 7 | No. 1 | 2 |
| 8 | No. 2 | 2 |
| 9 | No. 1 | 8 |
| 10 | No. 2 | 2 |
| 11 | No. 1 | 2 |
| 12 | No. 2 | 8 |
| 13 | No. 1 | 2 |
| 14 | No. 2 | 2 |
| 15 | No. 1 | 8 |
| 16 | No. 2 | 2 |
| 17 | No. 1 | 2 |

By following the steps outlined for weaving any one of the three plaid designs, you'll become aware of some of the possibilities of weaving designs with warp and weft stripes of varying sizes, creating a fabric with reversible designs. The possibilities are almost endless when you vary not only the size of the warp and weft stripes but also combine additional colors in both warp and weft. You could have two or more colors in the warp on each layer and use a wide variety of weft colors on each layer.

The three reversible plaid designs presented in this exercise are only three of the endless possibilities open to you. Once you understand the concept, you'll be able to create your own patterns in whatever proportions of warp and weft stripes suit your purpose. You need not be restricted to two colors, even on the two-color warp set up for these exercises; other colors could be easily introduced for the weft stripes. We used one of the warp colors as the continuous weft for one of the two sides of the fabric; we just as easily could have used a variety of other weft colors for one or for both sides. You can design warp for a reversible fabric with one, two, three, or more different colors for each layer. If the warp color arrangement for one layer is different from the warp color arrangement for the other layer, then reversing the layers in the weaving brings a different warp pattern to the surface. With a four-harness loom, double weave gives you two warp pattern possibilities, as two harnesses are required to weave each of the two warp patterns. Once the warp is threaded on the loom, those two warp patterns are established and can only be changed by rethreading.

The weft pattern possibilities are limited only by the number of wefts available to you; of course, you should also consider the relationship between the warp and weft colors and textures. In the weaving, you can decide how many weft colors you want to use for each layer. You can also decide how frequently you want to reverse the layers to give narrow, medium, or wide weft stripes. In the projects that follow, you'll find directions for weaving three throws or small blankets on a two-color warp arrangement, with the weft colors and the weft stripes different for each of the three. Exercise 17 is the last exercise in Part Two. Before taking the weaving off the loom, weave ½ in (1.3 cm), alternately raising harnesses 1 and 2 for one shot and harnesses 3 and 4 for the second shot.

## PROJECT 3:
# How to Weave Three Different Throws or Blankets on a Two-Color Double-Weave Warp

All the throws to be woven use the same warp arrangement, but the weft colors and the weft stripe patterns change for each throw. I wove this project using dark brown tweed and off-white as the warp colors; the weft colors included the warp colors, plus deep gold and burnt orange.

The warp is 40 in (101.6 cm) wide, with alternating stripes of color on each layer. Although the pattern of the warp stripes is the same on both layers, the color arrangement of the bottom layer is the reverse of the top layer. The diagram in Figure 27 shows the warp color arrangement for each layer. The colors are designated by letters (A,B,C,D, etc.) so that you may choose whatever colors you find most pleasing.

Each throw is about 80 in (203.2 cm) long, plus 6 in (15.2 cm) of fringe at each end. To figure the warp for each one: 80 in (203.2 cm) long plus 10 percent take-up in weaving = 88 in (223.5 cm) plus 6 in (15.2 cm) of fringe at each end, makes 100 in (254 cm)—or 88 + 12. Approximately 3 yd (108 in)—2.7 m (274.3 cm) should be allowed for weaving each throw. To weave three throws, 9 yd (8.2 m) of warp will be needed, plus 1 yd (0.9 m) of loom waste; therefore the warp will be 10 yd (9.1 m) long.

To weave only one or two throws, 3 yd (2.7 m) of warp length must be allowed for each one, and then the full loom waste must be added to that warp length. One throw would need 3 yd (2.7 m) plus 1 yd (0.9 m) loom waste or a total of 4 yd (3.6 m); two throws would need 6 yd (5.5 m) plus 1 yd (0.9 m) loom waste, or a total of 7 yd (6.4 m). Should your loom need more or less for loom waste, substitute the required amount in place of the 1 yd (0.9 m) loom waste, and adjust the yarn yardage requirements accordingly.

The yarn chosen for the project should be a softspun medium-weight wool, such as Marks Homespun from Ulltex or the Cum Homespun. Other yarns can work well as long as they will produce a woven product that is soft and drapable.

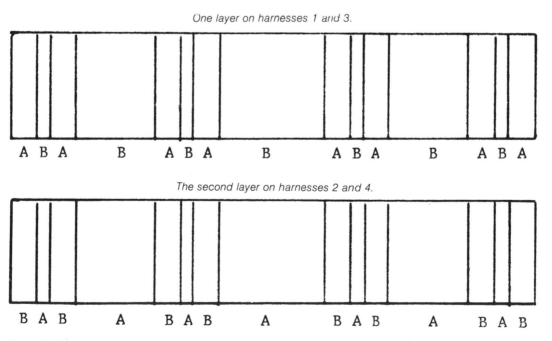

*One layer on harnesses 1 and 3.*

A B A     B     A B A     B     A B A     B     A B A

*The second layer on harnesses 2 and 4.*

B A B     A     B A B     A     B A B     A     B A B

Figure 27. *Warp color arrangement.*

## Figuring the Yarn Yardage for a 10-yd (9.1 m) Warp

Each layer of warp has eight threads of Homespun to the inch (2.5 cm) for 40 in (101.6 cm) or a total of 320 ends (8 × 40); the two layers will therefore have 640 ends (2 × 320). The upper layer has 16 in (40.6 cm) of color A and 24 in (61 cm) of color B; the bottom layer has 16 in (40.6 cm) of color B and 24 in (61 cm) of color A. Each color has a total of 40 in (101.6 cm) of warp ends for the two layers combined.

Color A. 40 in (101.6 cm) × 8 epi = 320 ends × 10 yd (9.1 m) long = 3200 yd (2912 m) warp yarn yardage needed

Color B. 40 in (101.6 cm) × 8 epi = 320 ends × 10 yd (9.1 m) long = 3200 yd (2912 m) warp yarn yardage needed

## MAKING THE WARP

If you're using a warping paddle to make the warp, work with spools in multiples of four or eight; alternate one spool of color A with one spool of color B four times—A, B, A, B, A, B, A, B—and you have ½ in (1.3 cm) of warp. If you can handle 16 ends in your paddle, eight of color A and eight of color B, alternating one by one, you can make 1 in (2.5 cm) of warp at a time.

If you don't use a paddle for warping, warp with one strand of color A and one strand of color B together to speed up making the warp.

*Threading the Loom.* Use a straight threading, with the top layer on harnesses 1 and 3 and the bottom layer on harnesses 2 and 4. The threading arrangement is as follows:

| Length of Warp | Number of Ends | Color | Harnesses | Layer |
|---|---|---|---|---|
| 2 in (5.1 cm) | 16 | A | 1 and 3 | top |
| | 16 | B | 2 and 4 | bottom |
| 1 in (2.5 cm) | 8 | B | 1 and 3 | top |
| | 8 | A | 2 and 4 | bottom |
| 2 in (5.1 cm) | 16 | A | 1 and 3 | top |
| | 16 | B | 2 and 4 | bottom |
| 6 in (15.2 cm) | 48 | B | 1 and 3 | top |
| | 48 | A | 2 and 4 | bottom |
| 2 in (5.1 cm) | 16 | A | 1 and 3 | top |
| | 16 | B | 2 and 4 | bottom |
| 1 in (2.5 cm) | 8 | B | 1 and 3 | top |
| | 8 | A | 2 and 4 | bottom |
| 2 in (5.1 cm) | 16 | A | 1 and 3 | top |
| | 16 | B | 2 and 4 | bottom |
| 8 in (20.3 cm) | 64 | B | 1 and 3 | top |
| | 64 | A | 2 and 4 | bottom |
| 2 in (5.1 cm) | 16 | A | 1 and 3 | top |
| | 16 | B | 2 and 4 | bottom |
| 1 in (2.5 cm) | 8 | B | 1 and 3 | top |
| | 8 | A | 2 and 4 | bottom |

| 2 in (5.1 cm) | 16 | A | 1 and 3 | top |
| | 16 | B | 2 and 4 | bottom |
| 6 in (15.2 cm) | 48 | B | 1 and 3 | top |
| | 48 | A | 2 and 4 | bottom |
| 2 in (5.1 cm) | 16 | A | 1 and 3 | top |
| | 16 | B | 2 and 4 | bottom |
| 1 in (2.5 cm) | 8 | B | 1 and 3 | top |
| | 8 | A | 2 and 4 | bottom |
| 2 in (5.1 cm) | 16 | A | 1 and 3 | top |
| | 16 | B | 2 and 4 | bottom |

Notice that the first two inches (5.1 cm) have 16 ends of color A on harnesses 1 and 3, with 16 ends of color B on harnesses 2 and 4. Count the first 32 ends on your lease sticks; there are 16 ends of color A, alternating one by one with 16 ends of color B. Take the first end of color A and thread it on harness 1; take the first end of color B and thread it on harness 2. The second end of color A is threaded on harness 3; the second end of color B is threaded on harness 4. Repeat this procedure until you've threaded the first 32 ends, thereby threading the first two inches (5.1 cm) of the top layer with color A and the first two inches (5.1 cm) of the bottom layer with color B.

The next inch (2.5 cm) has eight ends of color B on harnesses 1 and 3, with eight ends of color A on harnesses 2 and 4. Take the next 16 ends from the lease sticks and thread them, starting this time with the first end of color B on harness 1, followed by the first end of color A on harness 2. The second end of color B will go on harness 3, and the second end of color A will follow on harness 4. Repeat this procedure until you've threaded all 16 ends, thereby threading the one inch (2.5 cm) for the top layer with color B and the one inch (2.5 cm) of the bottom layer with color A.

Thread the rest of the warp the same way, noticing how many inches (or centimeters) are in each warp stripe and which color is used for each layer.

## To Sley the Reed

Use an eight-dent reed, two threads per dent, one of color A and one of color B.

## TO WEAVE PLAID THROW NO. 1

The weft colors for Plaid Throw No. 1 are the same colors used in making the warp, color A and color B: one side has color A as the continuous weft, while the other side has color B as the continuous weft. When harnesses 1 and 3 are used as the top warp layer with color A weft, solid blocks of color A occur where color A is threaded on harnesses 1 and 3, and mixed areas of color occur where color B is threaded on harnesses 1 and 3. When the layers of warp are switched and harnesses 2 and 4 are used as the top layer, the solid blocks of color occur, with the color A weft in the areas where color A is threaded on harnesses 2 and 4; in the areas where color B is threaded on harnesses 2 and 4, blocks of mixed colors occur. The width of the blocks of color remains the same, because that size is governed by the warp threading pattern. The height of the blocks of color depends on how frequently the layers are exchanged.

The weft stripe pattern for Plaid Throw No. 1 is given in Figure 28. The throw is 80 in (203.2 cm) long with 4-in (10.2-cm) stripes using harnesses 1 and 3 as the top layer, alternating with 2-in, 12-in, and 16-in (5.1-, 30.5-, and 40.6-cm) stripes, using harnesses 2 and 4 as the top layer of warp. The other side of the throw, woven with color B as the continuous weft, produces the identical pattern of blocks as the top layer, but the solid blocks of color are of color B.

The amount of weft yarn needed for each color can be determined by multiplying the number of inches (centimeters) of each color by the yardage needed to weave eight shots for each inch (to match the eight ends per inch). The warp is 40 in (101.6 cm) wide; allow 40 in (101.6 cm) of weft plus an additional 10 percent for take-up, or about 44 in (111.8 cm) needed for each weft shot. For ease in figuring the yardage, figure 4 ft (106.7 cm) for each weft shot × 8 shots per inch (2.5 cm), making 32 ft (976 cm), or approximately 11 yd (10 m) of weft yarn needed per inch (2.5 cm) on each layer.

80 in (203.2 cm) of color A (top layer) × 11 yd (10 m) = 880 yd (800.8 m) of color A weft

80 in (203.2 cm) of color B (bottom layer) × 11 yd (10 m) = 880 yd (800.8 m) of color B weft

Two treadling sequences are used; one has harnesses 1 and 3 as the top layer and the other has harnesses 2 and 4 as the top layer. The first treadling sequence is as follows:

*Step 1.* Raise harness 1. Weave one shot of color A.

*Step 2.* Raise harness 3. Weave one shot of color A.

*Step 3.* Raise harnesses 1 and 3 plus 2. Weave one shot of color B weft.

*Step 4.* Raise harnesses 1 and 3 plus 4. Weave one shot of color B weft.

The second treadling sequence is as follows:

*Step 1.* Raise harness 2. Weave one shot of color A.

*Step 2.* Raise harness 4. Weave one shot of color A.

*Step 3.* Raise harnesses 2 and 4 plus 1. Weave one shot of color B.

*Step 4.* Raise harnesses 2 and 4 plus 3. Weave one shot of color B weft.

Each treadling sequence weaves two rows on each layer of the warp. To weave Plaid Throw No. 1, follow the order of the treadling sequences as given below, weaving each sequence the number of inches (centimeters) specified on the list before going on to the next sequence.

**Figures 28–30** *(Left to right). Weft stripe patterns for Plaid Throw Nos. 1–3.*

This is the weft stripe sequence for Plaid Throw No. 1:

| Step | Treadling Sequence | Length |
|------|--------------------|--------|
| 1 | No. 1 | 4 in (10.2 cm) |
| 2 | No. 2 | 2 in (5.1 cm) |
| 3 | No. 1 | 4 in (10.2 cm) |
| 4 | No. 2 | 12 in (30.5 cm) |
| 5 | No. 1 | 4 in (10.2 cm) |
| 6 | No. 2 | 2 in (5.1 cm) |
| 7 | No. 1 | 4 in (10.2 cm) |
| 8 | No. 2 | 16 in (40.6 cm) |
| 9 | No. 1 | 4 in (10.2 cm) |
| 10 | No. 2 | 2 in (5.1 cm) |
| 11 | No. 1 | 4 in (10.2 cm) |
| 12 | No. 2 | 12 in (30.5 cm) |
| 13 | No. 1 | 4 in (10.2 cm) |
| 14 | No. 2 | 2 in (5.1 cm) |
| 15 | No. 1 | 4 in (10.2 cm) |

Be sure to leave 6 in (15.2 cm) of warp at the beginning and the end of your weaving to allow for the fringe. If you've made a warp long enough for two or three throws, weave 1 in (2.5 cm) in a different color before starting the next throw. Remember that you must again allow 6 in (15.2 cm) of warp for fringe for Plaid Throw No. 2.

## TO WEAVE PLAID THROW NO. 2

The weft colors for Plaid Throw No. 2 are color C in place of color A as the continuous weft for one side, with color B as the continuous weft for the other side. The side with color C weft will have blocks of mixed colors A and C, alternating with blocks of mixed colors B and C. The side with color B weft will have solid blocks of color B and blocks of mixed colors A and B.

The width of the blocks is again controlled by the warp threading pattern; the height of the blocks is again governed by the frequency of the exchange of the layers of warp threads.

The weft stripe pattern for Plaid Throw No. 2 is given in Figure 29. The throw is 79 in (200.7 cm) long, with 8-in (20.3-cm) and 3-in (7.6-cm) stripes using harnesses 1 and 3, alternating with 5-in (12.7-cm) stripes using harnesses 2 and 4 as the top layer of warp.

The amount of weft yarn needed for each color can be determined by multiplying the number of inches (centimeters) to be woven in each color by the yardage needed to weave eight shots for each inch (to match the eight ends per inch in the warp). The warp is 40 in (101.6 cm) wide; allow 40 in (101.6 cm) of weft plus an additional 10 percent for take-up, or about 44 in (111.8 cm) needed for each weft shot. For ease in figuring, allow 4 ft (106.7 cm) for each weft shot × 8 weft shots per inch (2.5 cm), making 32 ft (976 cm) or approximately 11 yd (10 m) of weft yarn needed per inch (2.5 cm) on each layer.

79 in (200.7 cm) of color C (top layer) × 11 yd (10 m) = 869 yd (790.8 m) of color C weft

79 in (200.7 cm) of color B (bottom layer) × 11 yd (10 m) = 869 yd (790.8 m) of color B weft

Two treadling sequences are used: one in which harnesses 1 and 3 produce the top layer, and the other in which harnesses 2 and 4 are used for the top layer. The first treadling sequence is as follows:

*Step 1.* Raise harness 1. Weave one shot of color C weft.

*Step 2.* Raise harness 3. Weave one shot of color C weft.

*Step 3.* Raise harnesses 1 and 3 plus 2. Weave one shot of color B weft.

*Step 4.* Raise harnesses 1 and 3 plus 4. Weave one shot of color B weft.

The second treadling sequence is as follows:

*Step 1.* Raise harness 2. Weave one shot of color C weft.

*Step 2.* Raise harness 4. Weave one shot of color C weft.

*Step 3.* Raise harnesses 2 and 4 plus 1. Weave one shot of color B weft.

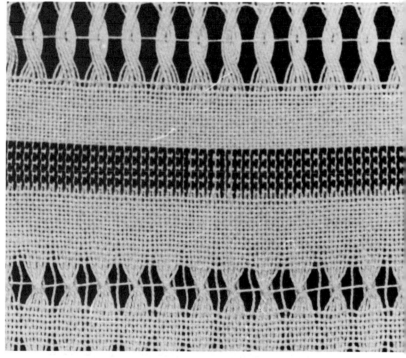

*Part One, Exercise Sampler.* (Left) At the bottom of the sampler, colors A and B interchange as the top layer. Next, two areas of lace are on top, seen against a bottom layer of plain weave. Above are stuffed tubes, some the full width of the warp, and others multiple tubes woven parallel to each other.

*Part One, Exercises 1 and 2.* (Top) In this detail of the sampler, color A (white) warp and weft was used for the top layer and color B (black) warp and weft for the bottom layer, then the colors were reversed.

*Part One, Exercises 4 and 5.* (Above) This detail of the sampler shows Brooks Bouquet lace (white) below, plain weave (black) beneath the lace, and leno lace above that, on a plain-weave background.

*Part One, Exercise 8.* (Right) These two tubes were woven simultaneously. By exchanging the warp colors and leaving the weft colors the same, you move the mixed color from the right-hand tube to the left-hand tube.

*Part One, Project 1.* (Below Left and Bottom) These pillows were woven by Judy Spark in four shades of green wool. The fringed pillow below has a closed hem at top and bottom and a slit in the middle of one side. The fringe is made from unwoven warp. The two pillows at the bottom of the page have closed hems; one opens at the top and the other on one side.

*Part One, Project 1.* (Left) This pillow is woven on a white wool warp with a blended black and white wool weft. The tubular weave has a slit in the middle of the top layer.

*Part One, Project 2.* (Below Left) Eileen Caruso models the wool bog shirt she wove on an 18-in (46-cm)-wide warp, with the same arrangement of colors on both layers of the warp. (Photo by Carole Shortt)

*Part Two, Exercises 13 through 15.* (Below Right) At the bottom, the two layers are stitched together with warp threads picked up at intervals from the lower layer. At the center, the initials PMW are picked up from the lower layer. At the top, a cross outlined by warp threads picked up from the bottom layer was stuffed as the weaving progressed, for an embossed or sculptural effect.

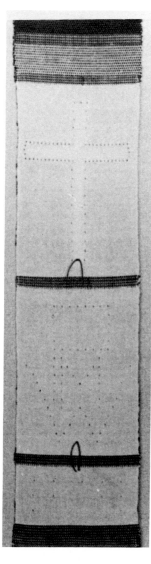

*Part Two, Exercise 17.* (Right) These reversible plaid designs were made on a warp threaded with varying widths of alternating stripes of color. By periodically reversing the layers or exchanging the two wefts, a variety of designs was produced.

*Part Two, Project 3.* (Below Left) Here, the contremarche loom is warped to weave reversible plaid throws, each 80 x 40 in (184 x 92 cm). The yarn is Swedish homespun wool in dark brown and off-white. (Bottom). Detail of finished plaid throw. (Photos by Carole Shortt)

*Part Two, Project 4.* (Left) Reversible twill rug, 20 x 42 in (57 x 107 cm); linen warp, Greek handspun wool weft. One shot of weft-faced twill alternates with one shot of warp-faced twill to give a weft-faced appearance to both sides of the rug.

*Part Three, Pick-Up Technique.* (Below) With white pattern threads on top of the pick-up stick and half the dark background warps raised, the shot is woven with the dark weft.

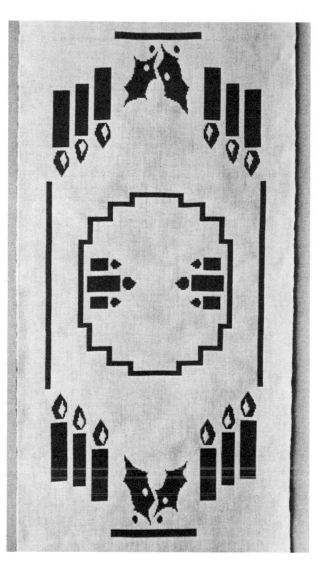

*Part Three, Exercise Sampler.* (Opposite Page, Far Left) This is the reverse side of the sampler. (Opposite Page, Left) This detail, showing the pick-up designs of Exercises 18 through 21, the sampler is turned to the side that was upright when it was woven.

*Part Three, Project 7.* (Above) Holiday table runner, designed and woven by Laurene Ouellette; 72 x 24 in (183 x 61 cm); 16/2 Swedish linen. On one side, the design is in red on a white background; on the other, the colors are reversed. (Photos by Carole Shortt)

*Part Three, Project 6; Homage to Lewis.* (Right) Warp-faced sculptural hanging, designed and woven by Palmy Weigle, 5 x 54 in (13 x 137 cm); 10/6 Swedish natural linen. (Below) Detail showing the finishing of the extra laid-in wefts added in Section 4. The 12 extra weft threads were used to make a tightly woven four-strand braid on each side of the piece.

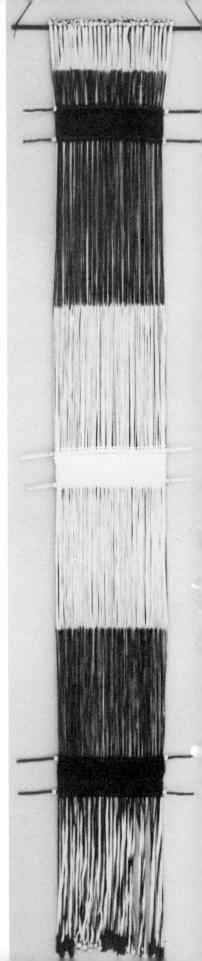

*Part Three, Project 5.* (Far Right) Crossed warp hanging, 60 x 8 in (152 x 20 cm), including the fringe at the top and bottom; No. 5 perle cotton in black and white. Chenille pipe cleaners were inserted at the top and bottom of each strip during weaving. To get the straight-line effect of the color change in the unwoven warp areas, a sword was inserted through the open side of the woven strips and pulled up or down to separate and straighten the layers of warp threads.

*Shirt.* (Top Left) Designed and woven by Klara Cherepov; 30-in (76-cm)-wide white wool warp with wool weft stripes. Woven tubular and double-width fabric was used for the sleeves and shoulders, and double-layered fabric for the neck opening.

*Vest.* (Above) Designed and woven by Jean Farley; 33 x 16 in (83 x 41 cm); 2/20 wool, mohair, and various novelty yarns as warp; variegated novelty yarn as weft. Trim is heavy rayon, woven in on every other shed. (Photo by Bill Swan)

*Lace Blouse.* (Left) Designed and modeled by Peggy A. Manja; 20 x 18 in (51 x 46 cm) tube; sports wool warp for the bottom layer, nub-type wool and cotton blend for the top-layer warp, and both yarns used randomly for the weft. Brooks Bouquet lace rows appear on front, back, and bodice. The sleeves were woven as separate tubes, with lace on the top layer only. A 6-in (15-cm) slit in the middle of the bottom layer makes the shoulders for the blouse. (Photo by Jan LaRoche)

*The Lord Is My Shepherd.* (Above)
Double-weave pick-up hanging woven by
Eva R. E. Quinn from an illustration on page
286 of *The Joy of Handweaving* by Osma
Gallinger Tod (2nd ed.). (Used by courtesy
of the author. Photo by the Quinn Studio)

*The Weaver's Creed.* (Above Right)
Double-weave pick-up hanging woven by
Eva R. E. Quinn from a design furnished
through the courtesy of Osma Gallinger Tod.
(Photo by the Quinn Studio)

*Saddle Bag.* (Right) Notice how the center
single-layer section is gathered in the
middle to create the handle for the bag.

*Raise Your Banner High.* (Top Left) Layered double-weave wall hanging, designed and woven by Jean Farley; 38 x 36 in (96 x 91 cm). The lower warp consists of four shades of red and rust rug wool; the upper warp is mixed gray rug wool and worsteds. The unused warp ends of the upper layer are finger-woven, braided, and wrapped. (Photo by Bill Swan)

*Wall Hanging.* (Left) Stylized tree design woven by Laurene Ouellette using the Pick-up technique; 22 x 28 in (56 x 71 cm); perle cotton.

*Wall Hanging.* (Above) Double-weave pick-up hanging, designed and woven by Lynn Fischer; 11 x 24 in (28 x 61 cm); wool. The bird is dark on a light background on one side, and light on a dark background on the other side.

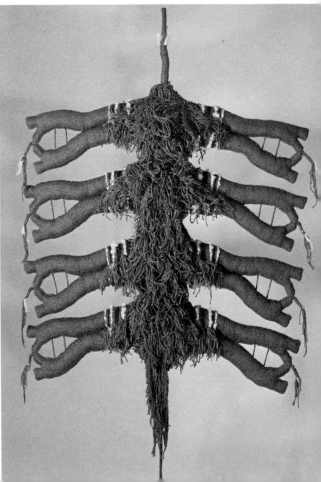

*Opposite Page: Four Ballerinas.* (Top Left) Fiber sculpture, designed and woven by Ruth Geneslaw; 61 x 28 in (155 x 71 cm); Tubular weave, rya; wool and unspun fleece; reinforced with metal rods. (Photo by Michael Smirnoff)

*Wheat.* (Top Right) Fiber sculpture, designed and woven by Ruth Geneslaw; 26 x 11 in (66 x 28 cm); tubular weave, rya, wrapping; linen. (Photo by Michael Smirnoff)

*Homage to Bryce Canyon.* (Lower Left) Fiber sculpture, designed and woven by Ruth Geneslaw; 54 x 44 x 30 in diameter (137 x 112 x 76 cm). Tubular weave and wrapping; wool and unspun fleece. (Photo by Michael Smirnoff)

*Cactus.* (Lower Right) Fiber sculpture, designed and woven by Ruth Geneslaw; 60 x 36 in (152 x 91 cm); tubular weave, rya wrapping; rayon and unspun flax; turned 90 degrees. (Photo by Michael Smirnoff)

*Glimpses.* (Top) Wall hanging by M. W. Little; 14 x 28 in (36 x 71 cm); 20/2 linen in pink, silver gray, and navy blue. Flat tapestry encased in Plexiglas to allow viewing from both sides. (Photo by David Planka)

*100 Views.* (Above) Tapestry by M. W. Little; 5 x 6 ft; wool in four shades of orange and four shades of blue. The tapestry was woven in four 14-in (36-cm)-wide strips with a different shade of orange and blue in each one. The strips were then sewn together halfway down the length.

*No Regrets: Glendora Ridge.* (Left) Tapestry by M. W. Little; 36 x 36 in (94 x 94 cm); tussah silk, one layer warp in a solid copper color; the other striped warm and cool grays. Same colors in weft. (Photo by David Planka)

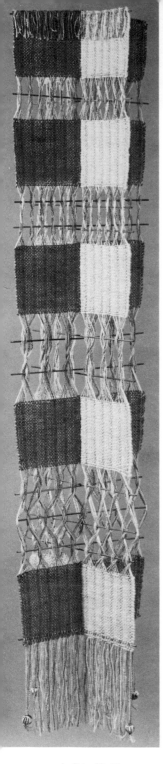

*Left to Right:*

*Bisecting Planes.* Mobile designed and woven by Jean Farley; 12 x 12 in (30 x 30 cm) wide x 58 in (147 cm) long; warp is white and natural mixed fibers, including bouclé; wefts are heavy jute. (Photo br Bill Swan)

*Double-Weave Sampler.* A variety of double-weave techniques are shown here.

*Crossed Warp Tubular Hanging.* Designed and woven by Jean Farley; 6 in (15 cm) in diameter x 60 in (152 cm) long; 2/20 wool worsted warp in mixed shades; weft is of various novelty fibers. (Photo by Bill Swan)

*Lace Wall Hanging.* Woven by Greta Klingenburg; 27 x 60 in (69 x 152 cm). A study incorporating a variety of lace patterns, including leno lace and Danish medallion. (Photo by Carole Shortt)

*Reversible Rug.* (Top) Handwoven in Mexico, owned by Palmy Weigle; 54 x 90 in (137 x 229 cm); white, gray, and black wool. (Photo by Carole Shortt)

*Wall Hanging.* (Above) Designed and woven by Chris Daley; 20 x 24 in (51 x 61 cm) plus fringe; one layer white wool; the other, variegated green. Pick-up double weave technique. (Left) Design threads of the white warp are being picked up during the weaving. (Photos by Chris Daley)

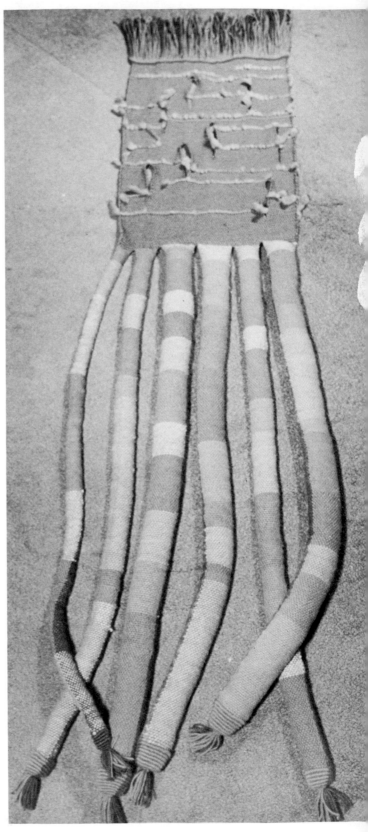

*Party Blower.* (Above) Tubular fiber sculpture, designed and woven by Malina Kern; 15 ft x 10 in (5 m x 25 cm) opened; 5 ft (1.5 m) long in coiled position; cotton warp with fleck mohair weft. Beads, feathers, and shells added to warp ends. Awarded First Prize for sculpture by the Westchester Art Society in 1973. (Photo by Doreen Bassin)

*Exploration.* (Right) Three-dimensional fiber sculpture, designed and woven by Dolly Curtis; 50-in (127-cm)-long tubes attached to a 4-ft (107-cm) single-layer fabric with preplanned slits. Rug wool and hand-dyed fleece. Knotted finish on the tubes. (Photo by Victor Cromwell)

*Step 4.* Raise harnesses 2 and 4 plus 3. Weave one shot of color B weft.

Each treadling sequence weaves two rows on each layer of warp. To weave Plaid Throw No. 2, follow the order of the treadling sequences as given below, weaving each sequence the number of inches (centimeters) specified on the list before going on to the next sequence.

This is the weft stripe sequence for Plaid Throw No. 2:

| Step | Treadling Sequence | Length |
|:---:|:---:|:---:|
| 1 | No. 1 | 8 in (20.3 cm) |
| 2 | No. 2 | 5 in (12.7 cm) |
| 3 | No. 1 | 3 in (7.6 cm) |
| 4 | No. 2 | 5 in (12.7 cm) |
| 5 | No. 1 | 8 in (20.3 cm) |
| 6 | No. 2 | 5 in (12.7 cm) |
| 7 | No. 1 | 3 in (7.6 cm) |
| 8 | No. 2 | 5 in (12.7 cm) |
| 9 | No. 1 | 3 in (7.6 cm) |
| 10 | No. 2 | 5 in (12.7 cm) |
| 11 | No. 1 | 8 in (20.3 cm) |
| 12 | No. 2 | 5 in (12.7 cm) |
| 13 | No. 1 | 3 in (7.6 cm) |
| 14 | No. 2 | 5 in (12.7 cm) |
| 15 | No. 1 | 8 in (20.3 cm) |

Be sure to leave 6 in (15.2 cm) of warp at the beginning and end of the weaving to allow for a fringe on each end. If you have a warp long enough for two or three throws, weave 1 in (2.5 cm) in a different color before starting the next throw.

## TO WEAVE PLAID THROW NO. 3

The weft colors for Plaid Throw No. 3 are color A as the continuous weft for one side, with color D in place of color B as the continuous weft for the other side. The side with the color A weft will have solid blocks of color A alternating with blocks of mixed colors A and B; the side with the color D weft will have blocks of mixed colors A and D alternating with blocks of mixed colors B and D. The width of the blocks is controlled, as usual, by the warp threading pattern; the height of the blocks will vary depending upon the frequency with which the layers of warp are exchanged.

The weft stripe pattern is given in Figure 30. The throw is 80 in (203.2 cm) long with ten 8-in (20.3-cm) stripes on each side, with 8 in (20.3 cm) using harnesses 1 and 3 as the top layer, alternating with 8 in (20.3 cm) using harnesses 2 and 4 as the top layer.

The amount of weft yarn needed for each color can be determined by multiplying the number of inches (centimeters) to be woven in each color by the yardage needed to weave eight shots per inch (to match the eight warp ends per inch). The warp is 40 in (101.6 cm) wide; allow 40 in (101.6 cm) of weft plus an additional 10 percent for take-up, or 44 in (111.8 cm) for each weft shot. For ease in figuring, allow 4 ft (106.7 cm) for each weft shot × 8 weft shots per inch (2.5 cm), making 32 ft (976 cm), or approximately 11 yd (10 m) of weft needed per inch (2.5 cm) on each layer.

80 in (203.2 cm) of color A (top layer) × 11 yd (10 m) = 880 yd (800.8 m) of color A weft yarn

80 in (203.2 cm) of color D (bottom layer) × 11 yd (10 m) = 880 yd (800.8 m) of color D weft yarn

Two treadling sequences are used, one using harnesses 1 and 3 for the top layer and the other using harnesses 2 and 4 for the top layer. The first treadling sequence is as follows:

*Step 1.* Raise harness 1. Weave one shot of color A.

*Step 2.* Raise harness 3. Weave one shot of color A.

*Step 3.* Raise harnesses 1 and 3 plus 2. Weave one shot of color D.

*Step 4.* Raise harnesses 1 and 3 plus 4. Weave one shot of color D weft.

The second treadling sequence is as follows:

*Step 1.* Raise harness 2. Weave one shot of color A weft.

*Step 2.* Raise harness 4. Weave one shot of color A weft.

*Step 3.* Raise harnesses 2 and 4 plus 1. Weave one shot of color D weft.

*Step 4.* Raise harnesses 2 and 4 plus 3. Weave one shot of color D weft.

Each treadling sequence weaves two rows on each layer of warp. To weave Plaid Throw No. 3, follow the order of the treadling sequences as given below, weaving each sequence the number of inches (centimeters) specified on the list before going on to the next sequence.

The weft stripe sequence for Plaid Throw No. 3 is as follows:

| Step | Treadling Sequence | Length |
|------|--------------------|--------|
| 1 | No. 1 | 8 in (20.3 cm) |
| 2 | No. 2 | 8 in (20.3 cm) |
| 3 | No. 1 | 8 in (20.3 cm) |
| 4 | No. 2 | 8 in (20.3 cm) |
| 5 | No. 1 | 8 in (20.3 cm) |
| 6 | No. 2 | 8 in (20.3 cm) |
| 7 | No. 1 | 8 in (20.3 cm) |
| 8 | No. 2 | 8 in (20.3 cm) |
| 9 | No. 1 | 8 in (20.3 cm) |
| 10 | No. 2 | 8 in (20.3 cm) |

Be sure to leave 6 in (15.2 cm) of warp at the beginning and the end of the weaving to allow for the fringe at each end of the throw.

# PROJECT 4:
# How to Weave a Double-Faced Twill Rug

Rugs can be woven using a number of double-weave techniques, such as reversible rugs in plain weave with different colors appearing on the two sides, or woven of interlocking layers with alternating weft colors on either side. The technique of Exercise 16, using alternating shots of weft-faced and warp-faced twills, lends itself especially to the production of strong, serviceable rugs.

Project 4 is a double-faced rug, 30 in (76.2 cm) wide by 60 in (152.4 cm) long, with the warp set far enough apart so that the weft can cover it completely. The weaving is a sequence of eight steps, one shot of weft-faced twill alternating with one shot of warp-faced twill, resulting in a weft-faced reversible rug, with the twill effect on both sides.

## MAKING THE WARP

The warp chosen for the project is a hard twist cotton, a No. 9 seine line or 8/4 carpet warp, or a firm 8/5 linen set at six ends to the inch (2.5 cm). To figure the amount of warp yarn needed, multiply the width, 30 in (76.2 cm), by six (the number of ends per inch), making 180 ends. Add three extra warp threads at each side to furnish firmness to the first ½ in (1.3 cm) at each selvedge of the rug.

180 ends + 6 selvedge threads = 186 total warp threads

To determine the length of the warp, figure the length of the rug at 60 in (152.4 cm), plus 10 percent take-up in weaving, makes 66 in (167.6 cm) of warp. Add 8 in (20.3 cm) at each end for a knotted or braided fringe; 66 in (167.6 cm) + 16 in (40.6 cm) = 82 in (208.3 cm) or 2 yd (1.8 m) and 10 in (25.4 cm). The loom waste of 1 yd (0.9 m) must then be added. If your loom requires more loom waste or less, substitute the correct amount and adjust the warp length accordingly.

66 in (167.6 cm) + 16 in (40.6 cm) + 36 in (77.7 cm) = 118 in (150 cm) or 3 yd (2.7 m) 10 in (25.4 cm) of warp length required

Make a warp 3½ yd (3.2 m) or 126 in (320 cm) long which will allow a few inches (centimeters) for practicing the technique and establishing an even beat in your weaving. To plan the amount of warp yarn yardage required, figure:

186 warp ends × 3½ yd (3.2 m) long = 651 yd (592.4 m) of warp-yarn yardage needed

*Threading the Warp.* Thread the first 7 warp ends as follows: 1–1, 2–2, 3–3, 4. In other words, the first warp end is threaded on the first heddle of harness 1, and the second warp end is threaded on the second heddle of harness 1. The third warp end is threaded on the first heddle of harness 2; the fourth end is threaded on the second heddle of harness 2. The fifth end is threaded on the first heddle of harness 3; the sixth end is threaded on the second heddle of harness 3; and the seventh end is threaded on harness 4. Use a straight threading, 1–2–3–4, for the rest of the warp until you reach the last seven warp ends. Thread the seventh from the last on harness 1, the next two on separate heddles on harness 2, then two on separate heddles on harness 3, with the last two on separate heddles on the fourth harness.

*Sleying the Warp.* Use a six-dent reed. The first six threads on each end will be sleyed two per dent and the rest of the warp will be sleyed one end per dent.

## Figuring the Weft Yarn

The yarn chosen for the weft is a heavy three-ply or four-ply rug wool capable of covering the warp completely. If medium-weight two-ply rug wool is more readily available to you, using a two-ply rug wool doubled or tripled can also give a good wearable surface for the rug.

Because the weft covers all the warp threads, the pattern is determined entirely by the color and size of the weft stripes. For this project, we are using two colors, with the weft stripes the same size on either side; the large center area is color A on one side and color B on the other side (see Figure 31). One side has 32 in (81.3 cm) of color A and 28 in (71.1 cm) of color B; the other side has 32 in (81.3 cm) of color B and 28 in (71.1 cm) of color A. Each color, therefore, is used for 60 in (152.4 cm) of weaving. Depending upon the firmness with which the weft shots are beaten, there will be eight to ten weft shots to the inch for each layer. To be on the safe side, figure ten weft shots to the inch (2.5 cm) for 60 in (152.4 cm), or a total of 600 weft shots of each color.

The width of the warp is 30 in (76.2 cm), but each weft shot needs an extra 10 percent or 3 in (7.6 cm) for take-up in weaving; 33 in (83.8 cm) or approximately 1 yd (0.9 cm) of heavy three-ply or four-ply rug wool is needed for each weft shot. At ten weft shots to the inch, 10 yd (9.1 m) of weft yarn are needed for each inch (2.5 cm) on each side of the rug.

60 in (152.4 cm) color A × 10 yd (9.1 m) per inch (2.5 cm) = 600 yd (1524 m) of color A weft yarn

60 in (152.4 cm) color B × 10 yd (9.1 m) per inch (2.5 cm) = 600 yd (1524 m) of color B weft yarn

## The Tie-Up and Treadling For the Loom

For a loom with six treadles, this eight-step treadling sequence can be achieved by the tie-up below:

| Treadle | 1 | 2 | 3 | 4 | 5 | 6 |
|---|---|---|---|---|---|---|
| Harnesses | 1 and 3 | 1 | 3 | 4 | 2 | 2 and 4 |

Two treadling sequences will be used for weaving the rug; the first will use color A for the top layer and color B for the bottom layer, while the second one will have

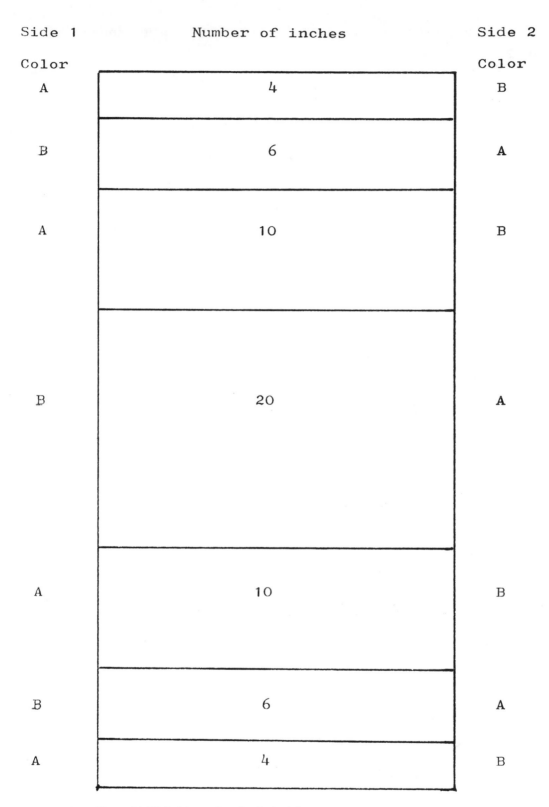

| Side 1 Color | Number of inches | Side 2 Color |
|:---:|:---:|:---:|
| A | 4 | B |
| B | 6 | A |
| A | 10 | B |
| B | 20 | A |
| A | 10 | B |
| B | 6 | A |
| A | 4 | B |

Figure 31. *Weft stripe pattern for Project 4.*

color B on top and color A on the bottom. The first treadling sequence is as follows:

*Step 1.* Raise harness 1. Weave one shot of color A.

*Step 2.* Raise harnesses 1–2–3. Weave one shot of color B.

*Step 3.* Raise harness 2. Weave one shot of color A.

*Step 4.* Raise harnesses 2–3–4. Weave one shot of color B.

*Step 5.* Raise harness 3. Weave one shot of color A.

*Step 6.* Raise harnesses 3–4–1. Weave one shot of color B.

*Step 7.* Raise harness 4. Weave one shot of color A.

*Step 8.* Raise harnesses 4–1–2. Weave one shot of color B.

The second treadling sequence is as follows:

*Step 1.* Raise harness 1. Weave one shot of color B.

*Step 2.* Raise harnesses 1–2–3. Weave one shot of color A.

*Step 3.* Raise harness 2. Weave one shot of color B.

*Step 4.* Raise harnesses 2–3–4. Weave one shot of color A.

*Step 5.* Raise harness 3. Weave one shot of color B.

*Step 6.* Raise harnesses 3–4–1. Weave one shot of color A.

*Step 7.* Raise harness 4. Weave one shot of color B.

*Step 8.* Raise harnesses 4–1–2. Weave one shot of color A.

Before starting the weaving for the rug, leave at least 8 in (20.3 cm) of warp unwoven to use for the fringe at that end of the rug. To weave the rug in the weft stripe sequence given in the diagram for this project, follow the order of the treadling sequences below, weaving each sequence the number of inches (centimeters) specified before going on to the next sequence.

| Step | Treadling Sequence | Length |
|:---:|:---:|:---:|
| 1 | No. 1 | 4 in (10.2 cm) |
| 2 | No. 2 | 6 in (15.2 cm) |
| 3 | No. 1 | 10 in (25.4 cm) |
| 4 | No. 2 | 20 in (51 cm) |
| 5 | No. 1 | 10 in (25.4 cm) |
| 6 | No. 2 | 6 in (15.2 cm) |
| 7 | No. 1 | 4 in (10.2 cm) |

These seven steps will weave the 60 in (152.4 cm) of the rug. Before cutting the rug off the loom, be sure to allow another 8 in (20.3 cm) for the fringe at this end of the rug. To finish the rug, knot three warp ends of the fringe together, close to the edge of the weaving, all across the fringe, or braid the fringe in a series of three-strand braids.

# PART THREE:

# PICK-UP DOUBLE WEAVE, CROSSED WARP HANGINGS, AND THREE-DIMENSIONAL FLAPS

The exercises in Part Three give instructions on how to make designs using the pick-up method on double weave, how to do crossed warp hangings, and how to make three-dimensional flaps using suspended warps.

To do the exercises in this part, prepare a warp 2 yd (1.8 m) long, following the directions in Part One. Again, the yarn should be a strong, smooth yarn in two colors, with a strong contrast. Thread the loom with color A on harnesses 1 and 3, and color B on harnesses 2 and 4. For warps 15 ends per inch for each layer, sley the warp, two per dent, in a 15-dent reed. For warps 16 ends per inch, sley the threads, four per dent, in an eight-dent reed.

If you make a 6-yd (5.4-m) warp to do the exercises in this book, you must cut off the reversible plaid design of Exercise 17 and rethread the loom. To prepare the loom for rethreading, follow the directions given at the beginning of Exercise 17. Once the plaid design is cut off, rethread the loom with color A on harnesses 1 and 3, and with color B on harnesses 2 and 4. Sley warps 15 ends per inch per layer with two ends per dent in a 15-dent reed. Sley warps 16 ends per inch per layer with four ends per dent in an eight-dent reed.

Before starting Exercise 18, weave ½ in (1.3 cm), alternately raising harnesses 1 and 3 for one shot and harnesses 2 and 4 for the second shot.

# EXERCISE 18:
# How to do the Basic Pick-Up Procedure With a Simplified Design

Using a warp threaded with a separate color on each layer, you can weave designs with a pattern in color A against a background in color B, or you can pick up a design in color B with a background in color A. For this exercise, the design will be in color B (on harnesses 2 and 4), and the background will be color A (on harnesses 1 and 3) on the top layer of the fabric.

The easiest designs to weave are those made of square or rectangular shapes. I've chosen a stylized tree (see Figure 32) in order to familiarize you with the basic procedure for doing pick-up designs. The tree was plotted to scale on graph paper, with each square representing two warp threads in width and two weft shots in height. The design at its widest point uses 48 warp threads (24 squares wide) and 72 weft shots (36 squares high).

The pattern is picked up in groups of two warp threads from the color B ends; the background is picked up in groups of two warp threads from the color A ends. Working over a stylized design, here a tree, you will weave a completely reversible design. The tree will be in color B on the top layer of the fabric and an identical tree will be in color A on the bottom layer.

The basic procedure for producing a pick-up design with color A as the

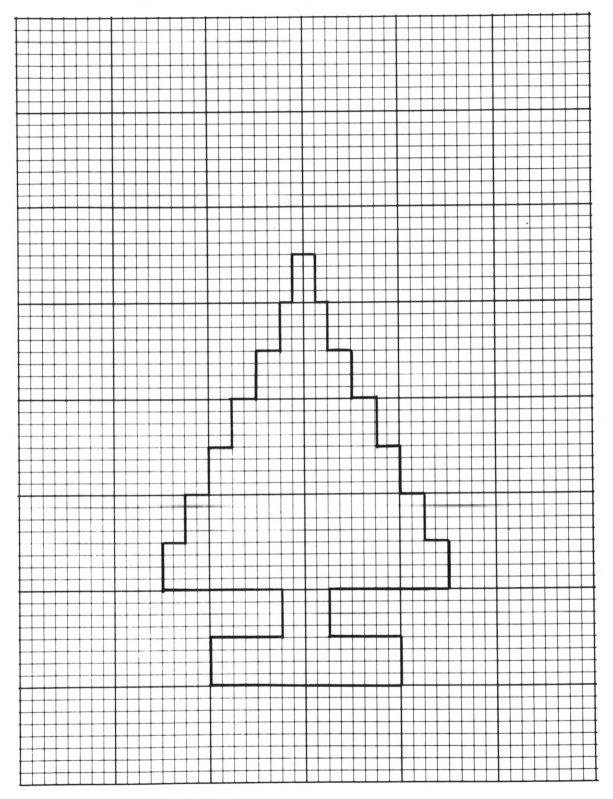

Figure 32. *Stylized tree design for pick-up procedure exercise.*

background and color B as the pattern is a sequence of eight steps as follows:

*Step 1.* Raise harnesses 2 and 4. Using a pick-up stick or a sword, pick up the pattern threads from the color B warp ends. (The specific warp ends for this design will be given in a separate list.) Lower harnesses 2 and 4. The pattern warps are now on top of the pick-up stick.

*Step 2.* Raise harness 1. Push the beater forward and then back to clear the shed. With the pattern warps still on top, push the pick-up stick back against the beater. Pass weft color A through the shed. Remove the pick-up stick and beat.

*Step 3.* Raise harnesses 1 and 3. Pick up the background warp threads from color A warp ends. Lower harnesses 1 and 3. The background color A warps are now on top of the pick-up stick. In picking up the background warps, the same number of warp color A ends are left below the stick as were picked up for the pattern in Step 1. In other words, if the center 10 color B ends were picked up for the pattern in Step 1, the warp ends picked up for the background would be all color A warps, except the center 10 color A ends; these center 10 color A ends would remain below the pick-up stick for Step 3.

*Step 4.* Raise harness 2. Push the beater forward, then back to clear the shed. Push the pick-up stick back against the beater. Pass color B weft through the shed. Remove the pick-up stick and beat.

*Step 5.* Raise harnesses 2 and 4. Pick up the same color B pattern warp ends as were picked up in Step 1. Lower harnesses 2 and 4.

*Step 6.* Raise harness 3. Push the beater forward and back to clear the shed. Pass weft color A through the shed. Remove the pick-up stick and beat.

*Step 7.* Raise harnesses 1 and 3. Pick up the same color A background warps as were picked up in Step 3. Lower harnesses 1 and 3.

*Step 8.* Raise harness 4. Push the beater forward and back to clear the shed. Push the pick-up stick back against the beater. Pass color B weft through the shed. Remove pick-up stick and beat.

This sequence of eight steps weaves two complete rows of the design on each layer of the fabric. As an aid in following the sequence for the weft color, notice that, when color B warp threads are on top of the pick-up stick, color A weft is used. In the same way, when color A warp threads are on top of the pick-up stick, color B weft is used.

Be sure to keep good tension on your warp to help create a better shed; if your loom doesn't give a clear shed, insert a sword in the shed before passing the weft shot through. Turn the sword on its side and keep it back against the reed to enable the weft thread to pass through, then remove both the pick-up stick and sword before beating. You may find that flat shuttles will work better than boat shuttles when doing pick-up designs.

## To Weave the Tree Design

Before starting the design, weave 1 in (2.5 cm) in two separate layers as follows:

Raise harness 1. Weave one shot of color A.
Raise harness 3. Weave one shot of color A.
Raise harnesses 1 and 3 plus 2. Weave one shot of color B.
Raise harnesses 1 and 3 plus 4. Weave one shot of color B.

Start with the color A shuttle at the right-hand selvedge and with color B at the left-hand selvedge. After weaving this first inch (2.5 cm), the color A shuttle should again be at the right-hand side and the color B at the left side. When you start weaving the eight-step sequence for the pick-up, if you start with color A at the right and color B at the left, one complete sequence will bring them back to their original positions. In this way, it will be easier for you to recognize when you've completed the eight-step sequence.

If you look at the tree design in Figure 32, you'll see that the first part of the design at the bottom (the stand for the tree) is 16 squares wide; each square represents two threads, making 16 squares equal to 32 warp threads. The same 32 warp threads are used for four squares in the height of the design; each square represents two weft rows for each layer, with four squares in height equal to eight weft rows for each layer. Remember that the complete sequence of eight steps previously outlined weaves two rows for each layer; therefore four repeats of the eight-step sequence are needed to weave eight weft rows for each layer.

The design for the next part of the tree (the trunk) is only four squares wide, or eight warp threads. This part is also four squares high and would require four repeats of the eight-step sequence in order to produce the eight weft rows represented by the four squares. Notice that the design has been laid out so that each part is four blocks in height in order to make it easier to weave this first pick-up design.

The warp threads used for the pattern and for the background of each section of the tree design are as follows:

| Section | Background Color A | Pattern Color B | Background Color A | Repeat Eight-Step Sequence |
|---------|--------------------|-----------------|--------------------|----------------------------|
| 1 | 44 (48) | 32 | 44 (48) | 4 times |
| 2 | 56 (60) | 8 | 56 (60) | 4 times |
| 3 | 36 (40) | 48 | 36 (40) | 4 times |
| 4 | 40 (44) | 40 | 40 (44) | 4 times |
| 5 | 44 (48) | 32 | 44 (48) | 4 times |
| 6 | 48 (52) | 24 | 48 (52) | 4 times |
| 7 | 52 (56) | 16 | 52 (56) | 4 times |
| 8 | 56 (60) | 8 | 56 (60) | 4 times |
| 9 | 58 (62) | 4 | 58 (62) | 4 times |

The numbers given in parentheses for the background color A warp threads should be used for warps with 128 threads for each layer of warp; the first numbers given should be used for warps with 120 ends per layer. For example, in Section 1, use 44 color A warp ends on either side of the color B pattern ends if your warp has 120 ends for each layer; use 48 color A warp ends on either side of the 32 color B pattern ends if your warp has 128 ends for each layer.

## To Weave Section 1 of the Design

*Step 1.* Raise harnesses 2 and 4 (color B warp ends). Find the middle of the raised warp threads. Take the 16 center right warp ends and the 16 center left warp ends and place them on top of the pick-up stick. To check that you have the center 32 ends (16 + 16), there should be 44 warp ends on either side that are not picked up from the color B warps (48 if you have 128 ends per layer). Take a thin thread of a different color and place it under the 32 center warp threads to serve as a guide for picking up the correct threads in weaving the rest of the design. Lower harnesses 2 and 4, leaving the pick-up stick in place.

*Step 2.* Raise harness 1. Clear the shed. Pass color A weft through the shed. Remove the pick-up stick and beat.

*Step 3.* Raise harnesses 1 and 3 (color A warp ends). Pick up 44 (48) color A warps starting at the right-hand selvedge and going toward the center. Skip over the center 32 warp ends and pick up the 44 (48) warp ends remaining as you go to the left-hand selvedge. Lower harnesses 1 and 3. There are 44 (48) color A warp ends on top of the pick-up stick at each end with the center of the stick passing over the center 32 warp threads.

*Step 4.* Raise harness 2. Clear the shed; pass color B weft through the shed. Remove the pick-up stick and beat.

*Step 5.* Raise harnesses 2 and 4. Pick up the same 32 center color B warp ends that you picked up in Step 1. Lower harnesses 2 and 4.

*Step 6.* Raise harness 3. Clear the shed; pass color A weft through the shed. Remove the pick-up stick and beat.

*Step 7.* Raise harnesses 1 and 3. Pick up the same 44 (48) color A background warps from each side that you picked up in Step 3. Lower harnesses 1 and 3.

*Step 8.* Raise harness 4. Clear the shed; pass color B weft through the shed. Remove the pick-up stick and beat.

With these eight steps, you have woven two rows of the design on each layer of the warp. Repeat three more times to weave six additional rows; you now have completed the weaving for Section 1 of the design.

To weave Sections 2 through 9, refer to the list just given for the number of pattern and background threads for each part. In Section 2, pick up the center eight color B warps for the pattern and the outer 56 (60) color A warps on each side for the background. For each part, weave through the entire eight-step sequence four times. Remember that if you start with the color A shuttle at the right-hand side and the color B shuttle at the left-hand side, when one sequence is completed, the color A shuttle will again be at the right-hand side and the color B shuttle again at the left-hand side. After you've finished Section 9, weave 1 in (2.5 cm) in two separate layers, as you did before starting Section 1.

Before starting the next exercise, weave ½ in (1.3 cm) by alternately raising harnesses 1 and 2 for one shot and harnesses 3 and 4 for the second shot.

# EXERCISE 19:

# How to use the Pick-Up Technique to Silhouette and Frame a Design

Exercise 19 again centers on the stylized tree design; the design appears this time in color A against a background in color B within a frame of color A on the top layer. The basic procedure for the pick-up remains the same in essence, but harnesses 1 and 3 (color A warps) are used to pick up the pattern, and harnesses 2 and 4 are used to pick up the background.

The design is laid out to scale using graph paper, with each square representing two warp threads in width and two weft shots in height (see Figure 33). The shaded area in the diagram is the background, to be woven with color B as the top layer. The tree design and the clear borders around the background will appear with color A as the top layer. The fabric will again be reversible, as in Exercise 18, with the identical pattern with the colors reversed appearing on the bottom layer.

The warp threads to be used for the pattern and for the background of this design are as follows:

| Section | Pattern Frame Color A | Background Color B | Pattern Tree Color A | Background Color B | Pattern Frame Color A |
|---|---|---|---|---|---|
| 1 | 24 (28) | 72 | | | 24 (28) |
| 2 | 24 (28) | 20 | 32 | 20 | 24 (28) |
| 3 | 24 (28) | 32 | 8 | 32 | 24 (28) |
| 4 | 24 (28) | 12 | 48 | 12 | 24 (28) |
| 5 | 24 (28) | 16 | 40 | 16 | 24 (28) |
| 6 | 24 (28) | 20 | 32 | 20 | 24 (28) |
| 7 | 24 (28) | 24 | 24 | 24 | 24 (28) |
| 8 | 24 (28) | 28 | 16 | 28 | 24 (28) |
| 9 | 24 (28) | 32 | 8 | 32 | 24 (28) |
| 10 | 24 (28) | 34 | 4 | 34 | 24 (28) |
| 11 | 24 (28) | 72 | | | 24 (28) |

The first numbers given for the color A ends to be picked up for the frame pattern should be used for warps which have 120 ends for each layer; the numbers given in parentheses for the frame pattern ends should be used for warps which have 128 ends for each layer of warp. Sections 1 and 11 are each six squares in height on the diagram, representing 12 weft rows on each layer; six repeats of the eight-step sequence are needed to weave the 12 rows for each layer in Sections 1

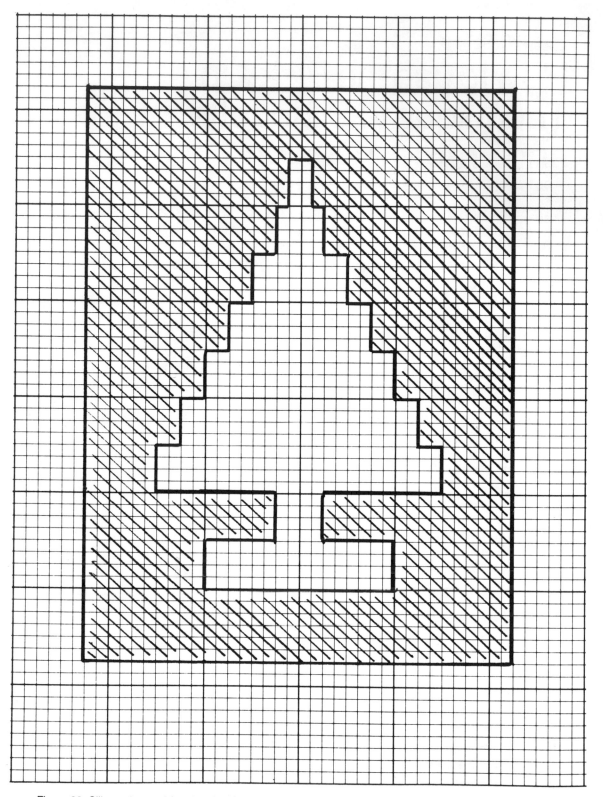

Figure 33. *Silhouetting and framing the design on graph paper.*

and 11. Sections 2 through 10 are four squares in height for each part; four repeats of the eight-step sequence are needed to weave the eight rows represented by the four squares.

## TO WEAVE THE TREE DESIGN

Before starting the pick-up for the design, weave 1½ in (3.8 cm) in two separate layers as follows:

Raise harness 1. Weave one shot of color A.
Raise harness 3. Weave one shot of color A.
Raise harnesses 1 and 3 plus 2. Weave one shot of color B.
Raise harnesses 1 and 3 plus 4. Weave one shot of color B.

Start with the color A shuttle at the right-hand side and the color B shuttle at the left-hand side; when you finish weaving 1½ in (3.8 cm), shuttle A will be back at the right-hand side and shuttle B back at the left-hand side. When you start weaving the eight-step sequence for the pick-up, if you start with color A at the right and color B at the left-hand side, one complete sequence will bring the shuttles back to their original positions. In this way, it will be easier for you to recognize when you have completed the eight-step sequence.

*Step 1.* Raise harnesses 1 and 3. Using a pick-up stick, pick up the first 24 (28) color A warp threads at the right-hand side, then pass the stick over the next 72 ends and pick up the 24 (28) color A ends at the left-hand side. Lower harnesses 1 and 3.

*Step 2.* Raise harness 2. Clear the shed by pushing the beater back and forth with the pick-up stick still in place. Pass color B weft through the shed. Remove the pick-up stick and beat.

*Step 3.* Raise harnesses 2 and 4. Pass the pick-up stick over the first 24 (28) color B warp ends and pick up the center 72 color B ends. The pick-up stick then passes over the remaining 24 (28) color B threads. Lower harnesses 2 and 4.

*Step 4.* Raise harness 1. Clear the shed. Pass color A weft through the shed. Remove the pick-up stick and beat.

*Step 5.* Raise harnesses 1 and 3. Pick up the same color A warp ends that you picked up in Step 1. Lower harnesses 1 and 3.

*Step 6.* Raise harness 4. Clear the shed. Pass color B weft through the shed. Remove the pick-up stick and beat.

*Step 7.* Raise harnesses 2 and 4. Pick up the same color B background warp ends that you picked up in Step 3. Lower harnesses 2 and 4.

*Step 8.* Raise harness 3. Clear the shed. Pass color A weft through the shed. Remove the pick-up stick and beat.

This sequence of eight steps weaves two rows of the design on each layer of the fabric. Section 1 is six squares or 12 rows in height. Repeat the eight-step sequence five more times to add the 10 rows needed to complete Section 1.

## Section 2

*Step 1.* Raise harnesses 1 and 3. Using a pick-up stick, pick up the first 24 (28) color A warp threads at the right-hand side; pass the stick over the next 32 color A ends and pick up the center 32 color A ends for the base of the tree design. Next pass the stick over 32 ends and pick up the last 24 (28) color A warp ends at the left-hand side. Lower harnesses 1 and 3. Color A ends are above the pick-up stick at each side for the frame and in the center for the tree.

*Step 2.* Raise harness 2. Clear the shed by pushing the beater back and forth; the pick-up stick is then pushed back toward the beater. Pass the color B weft through the shed; remove the pick-up stick and beat.

*Step 3.* Raise harnesses 2 and 4. Pass the pick-up stick over the first 24 (28) color B warp ends, then pick up 20 color B ends. Pass over the center 32 ends and pick up the next 20 color B ends. The end of the pick-up stick also passes over the last 24 (28) ends at the left-hand side. Lower harnesses 2 and 4. Color B ends are above the pick-up stick on either side of the center 32 ends, 20 on the right-hand side and 20 on the left-hand side.

*Step 4.* Raise harness 1. Clear the shed. Pass color A weft through the shed. Remove the pick-up stick and beat.

*Step 5.* Raise harnesses 1 and 3. Pick up the same color A warp ends that you picked up in Step 1. Lower harnesses 1 and 3.

*Step 6.* Raise harness 4. Clear the shed. Pass the color B weft through the shed. Remove the pick-up stick and beat.

*Step 7.* Raise harnesses 2 and 4. Pick up the same color B background warp ends that you picked up in Step 3. Lower harnesses 2 and 4.

*Step 8.* Raise harness 3. Clear the shed. Pass the color A weft through the shed. Remove the pick-up stick and beat.

With this eight-step sequence, you've woven two rows of the design on each layer of the fabric. Section 2 is four squares in height or eight weft rows on each layer. Repeat the eight-step sequence three more times to add the six rows needed to complete Section 2.

## Sections 3 Through 10

Each part is four squares or eight weft rows in height on each layer. Follow the weaving procedure as outlined for weaving Section 2, but use the correct warp ends for each part as specified on the list given above for the warp ends to be used for the pattern and the background of the pick-up design. For example, in Section 3, the ends to be picked up for the frame at each side remain the same, but there are only eight center color A warps to be picked up for the tree design. In Section 3, there are 32 color B warp ends to be picked up for the background on either side of the center eight ends. Weave through the eight-step sequence four times, using the designated pattern and background ends to produce the eight weft rows needed for each layer in Section 3.

Sections 4 through 10 will also require weaving through the eight-step sequence four times for each part, using the pattern and background ends designated on the list.

## Section 11

Section 11 is six squares in height or 12 weft rows for each layer. The same ends are used for the pattern and the background as were used in Section 1. Repeat the weaving procedure exactly as outlined for Section 1 to produce the 12 rows needed for each layer in Section 11. After you complete Section 11, weave 1½ in (3.8 cm) in two separate layers, using the treadling sequence given for the 1½ in (3.8 cm) woven before starting the pick-up for the design in this exercise.

Before starting the next exercise, weave ½ in (1.3 cm), alternately raising harnesses 1 and 2 for one shot and harnesses 3 and 4 for the second shot.

---

# EXERCISE 20:
# How to Plan and Weave a Circular Pick-Up Design

---

The designs used so far for the pick-up technique have been made with straight horizontal or vertical lines, the easiest designs to plot in warp threads and weft shots. Exercise 20 uses a circle 4 in (10 cm) in diameter as the pattern to be picked up in color B warp ends against a background of color A warp ends on the top layer of the fabric. A reverse version of the design appears on the bottom layer of the fabric.

## PLANNING THE DESIGN

Designs should be plotted to scale on graph paper. If you use graph paper with eight squares to the inch (2.5 cm) and each square represents two warp threads in width, each inch (2.5 cm) of the graph will be equal to 16 warp threads. Draw a circle on the graph paper with the circle 4 in (10 cm) or 32 squares wide at its widest point (see Figure 34). The curved line of the circle doesn't give a clear definition of how many threads in the warp should be picked up nor how many rows should be woven for each area of the design. The design must be squared up using the lines of the individual squares to plot a design that will create the illusion of a circle.

Start at the bottom and draw a line at the bottom of an area six squares wide; then draw a line at each end of the six squares going up one square in height. The bottom of the circle will therefore be six squares wide or 12 warp ends (two ends per square × 6). Each square represents two weft rows in height for each layer of the fabric; to weave the bottom area of the circle, weaving through the eight-step pick-up sequence once would produce the two weft rows per layer (Figure 35).

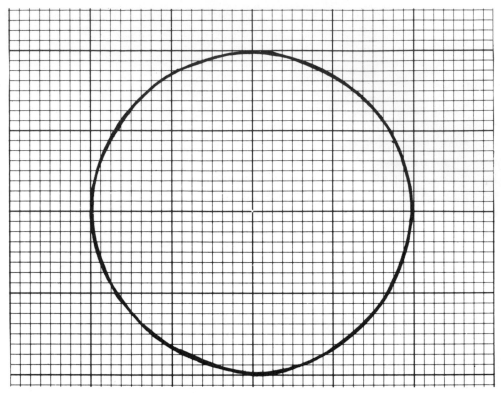

**Figure 34.** *Drawing a circle on graph paper.*

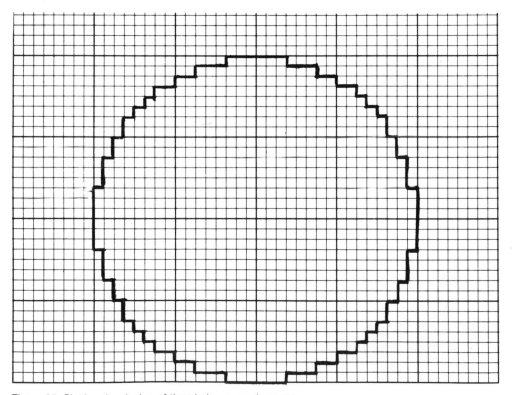

**Figure 35.** *Plotting the design of the circle on graph paper.*

Next draw lines at the bottom of the second row of squares going out three squares to the right and to the left of the six center squares already outlined. These squares should also be one square in height.

As the circle curves upward, the third row of squares will go out only two squares to the right and to the left of the previous row; this row is also one square in height. The fourth row goes out two more squares to the right and to the left and up one square high. The fifth and sixth rows go out one square each to the right and to the left; each row is one square in height. The curve of the circle becomes sharper now; rows 7 and 8 are the same in width, one square wider on each side than row 6. Rows 9 and 10 are also the same width, one square wider on each side than rows 7 and 8.

The circle climbs even more sharply; in squaring up the line, rows 11, 12, and 13 are the same in width, one square wider than rows 9 and 10. The design is now approaching the outer edges of the circle and should be as tall at the perimeter on each side as it is wide at the bottom. The next six rows, rows 14 through 19, are all the same width, 32 squares or 4 in (10 cm) wide.

The next three rows, rows 20 through 22, are all one square less in width on each side, 30 squares wide. Rows 23 and 24 are the same width, decreasing one square on each side as the line of the circle curves toward the top. Rows 25 and 26 decrease one more square on each side, and are 26 squares wide. With rows 27 and 28, the circle continues to become smaller as each row is one less square in width on each side. Rows 29 and 30 each decrease two squares on each side as the line of the circle begins to approach the top. Row 31 decreases by three squares on each side, 12 squares wide, just as row 2 is. Row 32 is the last row, six squares wide, the same as row 1.

When the circle is woven using the warp threads and the weft rows corresponding to the squared-up design, the pattern produced will give the illusion of a circle.

## TO WEAVE THE CIRCLE PATTERN IN COLOR B WITH COLOR A BACKGROUND

The warp threads to be used for the pattern and for the background are as follows:

| Row | Background Color A | Pattern Color B | Background Color A | Repeat Eight-Step Sequence |
|---|---|---|---|---|
| 1 | 54 (58) | 12 | 54 (58) | 1 time |
| 2 | 48 (52) | 24 | 48 (52) | 1 time |
| 3 | 44 (48) | 32 | 44 (48) | 1 time |
| 4 | 40 (44) | 40 | 40 (44) | 1 time |
| 5 | 38 (42) | 44 | 38 (42) | 1 time |
| 6 | 36 (40) | 48 | 36 (40) | 1 time |
| 7–8 | 34 (38) | 52 | 34 (38) | 2 times |
| 9–10 | 32 (36) | 56 | 32 (36) | 2 times |
| 11–13 | 30 (34) | 60 | 30 (34) | 3 times |
| 14–19 | 28 (32) | 64 | 28 (32) | 6 times |
| 20–22 | 30 (34) | 60 | 30 (34) | 3 times |

| | | | | |
|---|---|---|---|---|
| 23–24 | 32 (36) | 56 | 32 (36) | 2 times |
| 25–26 | 34 (38) | 52 | 34 (38) | 2 times |
| 27 | 36 (40) | 48 | 36 (40) | 1 time |
| 28 | 38 (42) | 44 | 38 (42) | 1 time |
| 29 | 40 (44) | 40 | 40 (44) | 1 time |
| 30 | 44 (48) | 32 | 44 (48) | 1 time |
| 31 | 48 (52) | 24 | 48 (52) | 1 time |
| 32 | 54 (58) | 12 | 54 (58) | 1 time |

The numbers given for the warp threads to be picked up for the background are for 120 threads to the inch (2.5 cm) and 128 threads to the inch (2.5 cm); the first number is for 120 ends per inch (2.5 cm), and the numbers in parentheses are for 128 ends per inch (2.5 cm).

The eight-step sequence to use for this exercise is as follows:

*Step 1.* Raise harnesses 2 and 4. Pick up the pattern threads from the color B warps. (For row 1, pick up 12 ends.) Lower harnesses 2 and 4.

*Step 2.* Raise harness 1. Clear the shed. Pass the color A weft through the shed. Remove the pick-up stick and beat.

*Step 3.* Raise harnesses 1 and 3. Pick up the background warp threads from the color A warp threads. (For row 1, pick up 54 (58) threads on either side of the center 12 warp ends.) Lower harnesses 1 and 3.

*Step 4.* Raise harness 2. Clear the shed. Pass the color B weft through the shed. Remove the pick-up stick and beat.

*Step 5.* Raise harnesses 2 and 4. Pick up the same color B pattern ends that you picked up in Step 1. Lower harnesses 2 and 4.

*Step 6.* Raise harness 3. Clear the shed. Pass the color A weft through the shed. Remove the pick-up stick and beat.

*Step 7.* Raise harnesses 1 and 3. Pick up the same color A background warps that you picked up in Step 3. Lower harnesses 1 and 3.

*Step 8.* Raise harness 4. Clear the shed. Pass the color B weft through the shed. Remove the pick-up stick and beat.

One complete sequence of eight steps weaves two rows on each layer of the fabric. Use the list to determine which pattern ends and which background ends should be picked up for each row; weave the eight-step sequence the required number of times as specified on the list.

Before you start weaving row 1, weave 1 in (2.5 cm) in two separate layers as follows:

Raise harness 1. Weave one shot of color A.
Raise harness 3. Weave one shot of color A.
Raise harnesses 1 and 3 plus 2. Weave one shot of color B.
Raise harnesses 1 and 3 plus 4. Weave one shot of color B.

Weave rows 1 through 32. Next weave 1 in (2.5 cm) in two separate layers using the same sequence just given.

Before starting the next exercise, weave ½ in (1.3 cm), alternately raising harnesses 1 and 2 for the first shot and harnesses 3 and 4 for the second shot.

# EXERCISE 21:

# How to Adapt a Free-Form Design to the Pick-Up Technique

The circle used for the pattern in Exercise 20 served to show how a curved line could be squared up for weaving as a pick-up design; however, the circle had a regularity to it in that the line of the curve was identical on both the right and left-hand sides. The free-form design for this exercise is a grouping of four petals, each one slightly different from the others (see Figure 36).

When planning a free-form design for use in the pick-up technique, use sketch paper to work out the design the way you want it to be. While you don't necessarily have to draw the design full size, the sketch should be made to scale. In other words, if the overall dimensions of the design are 30 × 40 in (76 × 102 cm), you could sketch to scale at 15 × 20 in (38 × 51 cm) or even 3 × 4 in (8 × 10 cm). Once you decide on the final form of the design, the pattern must be transferred to graph paper to plan the weaving.

The finer the graph paper used, the more subtle can be the development of the design. If each square on the graph represents 10 threads in the warp, obviously, strong horizontal or vertical lines would result when transferring the design, thus taking away from the free flow of the pattern. Using graph paper with each square representing two warp threads in width and two weft shots in height will permit very gradual changes in the lines of the design, thereby helping to maintain a smooth flow in the outline of the pattern.

Transfer the petal design to graph paper using two warp threads and two weft shots per square (see Figure 37). Then outline each petal on the graph using the squares that most closely conform to the shape of the petal. Outline lightly at first, as you may not always be satisfied with the first attempt. Sometimes having two rows increase two squares each will fit in better with the overall design than having one row increase one square and the next increase three squares. Bear in mind that each time you add one square to a row, you're adding two warp threads to the width. Each time two rows in succession are the same in width, you're adding four weft shots to that part of the design. Once you're satisfied with the progression of the lines, mark the outline so that you can read it easily.

The next step is to determine which warp threads are represented by the squares outlined on each row. The diagram in Figure 37 is 60 squares wide; at two

Figure 36. *Free-form design of four petals.*

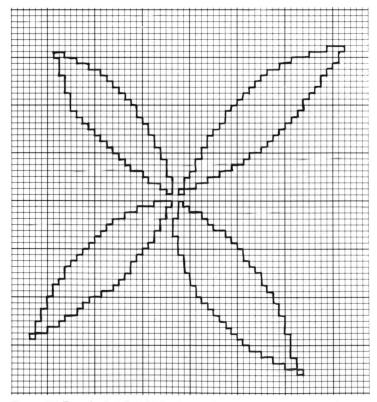

Figure 37. *Transferring the design to graph paper.*

warp threads per square, the width of the diagram represents the width of the warps set at 120 warp ends per layer. The first row of the design to be woven in pick-up is at the bottom of the design and is only one square wide or two warp threads; the number of pattern threads for row 1 is therefore two warp threads. There are 11 squares to the right of the pattern square; these 11 squares represent 22 background threads at the right-hand selvedge. There are 48 squares to the left of the pattern square or 96 warp ends for the background. If the pattern is to be picked up in color A and the background in color B, the directions for row 1 would read as follows:

| Background Color B Ends | Pattern Color A Ends | Background Color B Ends |
|:---:|:---:|:---:|
| 96 | 2 | 22 |

For warps with 128 ends per layer, there would be 100 color B ends for the background at the left, two pattern ends of color A, and 26 color B background ends at the right.

Row 2 has 12 squares for background at the right (14 for the 128 thread warps) or 24 color B warps (28 for the 128 thread warps); there are two pattern squares or four color A ends with 46 (48) squares to the left representing 92 (96) color B background threads. There are 55 rows to this design; each row should be analyzed in the same way as rows 1 and 2, and the correct number of warp ends noted for the pattern and for the background.

The list with the number of ends to be picked up should be as follows:

| Row | Background Color B | Pattern Color A | Background Color B | Pattern Color A | Background Color B |
|:---:|:---:|:---:|:---:|:---:|:---:|
| 1 | 96 (100) | | | 2 | 22 (26) |
| 2 | 92 (96) | | | 4 | 24 (28) |
| 3 | 88 (92) | | | 8 | 24 (28) |
| 4 | 84 (88) | | | 10 | 26 (30) |
| 5 | 80 (84) | | | 14 | 26 (30) |
| 6 | 78 (82) | | | 16 | 26 (30) |
| 7 | 6 (10) | 2 | 68 | 18 | 26 (30) |
| 8 | 8 (12) | 4 | 62 | 18 | 28 (32) |
| 9 | 8 (12) | 8 | 56 | 20 | 28 (32) |
| 10 | 10 (14) | 8 | 52 | 22 | 28 (32) |
| 11 | 10 (14) | 12 | 46 | 22 | 30 (34) |
| 12 | 12 (16) | 12 | 42 | 24 | 30 (34) |
| 13 | 12 (16) | 14 | 38 | 24 | 32 (36) |
| 14 | 14 (18) | 16 | 32 | 26 | 32 (36) |
| 15 | 14 (18) | 20 | 28 | 24 | 34 (38) |
| 16 | 16 (20) | 20 | 24 | 24 | 36 (40) |
| 17 | 18 (22) | 20 | 22 | 24 | 36 (40) |
| 18 | 18 (22) | 22 | 18 | 24 | 38 (42) |
| 19 | 20 (24) | 20 | 18 | 22 | 40 (44) |
| 20 | 22 (26) | 20 | 16 | 20 | 42 (46) |
| 21 | 24 (28) | 20 | 12 | 22 | 42 (46) |

| | | | | | |
|---|---|---|---|---|---|
| 22 | 26 (30) | 20 | 10 | 20 | 44 (48) |
| 23 | 28 (32) | 20 | 8 | 18 | 46 (50) |
| 24 | 30 (34) | 18 | 6 | 18 | 48 (52) |
| 25 | 32 (36) | 18 | 4 | 14 | 52 (56) |
| 26 | 34 (38) | 16 | 4 | 12 | 54 (58) |
| 27 | 38 (42) | 14 | 4 | 8 | 56 (60) |
| 28 | 42 (46) | 10 | 4 | 4 | 60 (64) |
| 29 | 48 (52) | 6 | 2 | 2 | 62 (66) |
| 30 | 120 color B warp ends | | | | |
| 31 | 52 (56) | 2 | 2 | 2 | 62 (66) |
| 32 | 50 (54) | 4 | 4 | 4 | 58 (62) |
| 33 | 46 (50) | 8 | 4 | 8 | 54 (58) |
| 34 | 44 (48) | 8 | 8 | 10 | 50 (54) |
| 35 | 40 (44) | 12 | 10 | 12 | 46 (50) |
| 36 | 38 (42) | 14 | 10 | 16 | 42 (46) |
| 37 | 36 (40) | 14 | 14 | 16 | 40 (44) |
| 38 | 34 (38) | 16 | 14 | 20 | 36 (40) |
| 39 | 32 (36) | 16 | 18 | 20 | 34 (38) |
| 40 | 30 (34) | 18 | 18 | 22 | 32 (36) |
| 41 | 28 (32) | 18 | 22 | 22 | 30 (34) |
| 42 | 26 (30) | 20 | 24 | 22 | 28 (32) |
| 43 | 24 (28) | 20 | 28 | 22 | 26 (30) |
| 44 | 22 (26) | 20 | 30 | 24 | 24 (28) |
| 45 | 20 (24) | 22 | 32 | 24 | 22 (26) |
| 46 | 20 (24) | 20 | 36 | 22 | 22 (26) |
| 47 | 20 (24) | 18 | 40 | 22 | 20 (24) |
| 48 | 18 (22) | 18 | 44 | 22 | 18 (22) |
| 49 | 18 (22) | 16 | 48 | 22 | 16 (20) |
| 50 | 18 (22) | 14 | 52 | 20 | 16 (20) |
| 51 | 16 (20) | 14 | 56 | 20 | 14 (18) |
| 52 | 16 (20) | 10 | 64 | 18 | 12 (16) |
| 53 | 16 (20) | 6 | 72 | 16 | 10 (14) |
| 54 | 14 (18) | 4 | 82 | 10 | 10 (14) |
| 55 | 106 (110) | | | 6 | 8 (12) |

The first numbers given for the color B background ends to be picked up at each side are for warps at 120 ends per layer; the numbers in parentheses are for warps with 128 ends per layer.

Notice that row 30 is made up entirely of color B warp ends. To weave row 30, weave two rows on each layer as follows:

Raise harness 2. Weave one shot of color B weft.
Raise harness 4. Weave one shot of color B weft.
Raise harnesses 2 and 4 plus 1. Weave one shot of color A weft.
Raise harnesses 2 and 4 plus 3. Weave one shot of color A weft.

This same four-step sequence should be used to weave 1 in (2.5 cm) in two separate layers before beginning the pick-up design.

After weaving this first inch (2.5 cm), which brings color B warp and weft to the top layer, you are ready to start weaving the pick-up design. Each row is one square in height, representing two weft shots for each layer of the fabric. Weave through the following eight-step sequence once for each row except row 30, referring to the list for the correct pattern and background warp threads to be picked up for each row.

The eight-step sequence for the petal design in color A with the background in color B is as follows:

*Step 1.* Raise harnesses 1 and 3. Pick up the pattern warps for the row. Lower harnesses 1 and 3.

*Step 2.* Raise harness 2. Clear the shed. Pass the color B weft through the shed. Remove the pick-up stick and beat.

*Step 3.* Raise harnesses 2 and 4. Pick up the background warp ends for this row. Lower harnesses 2 and 4.

*Step 4.* Raise harness 1. Clear the shed. Pass the color A weft through the shed. Remove the pick-up stick and beat.

*Step 5.* Raise harnesses 1 and 3. Pick up the same color A warp ends that you picked up in Step 1. Lower harnesses 1 and 3.

*Step 6.* Raise harness 4. Clear the shed. Pass the color B weft through the shed. Remove the pick-up stick and beat.

*Step 7.* Raise harnesses 2 and 4. Pick up the same color B warp ends that you picked up in Step 3. Lower harnesses 2 and 4.

*Step 8.* Raise harness 3. Clear the shed. Pass the color A weft through the shed. Remove the pick-up stick and beat.

Weave through each row in turn, picking up the correct warp threads as specified on the list. Notice that, beginning with row 7, a background area will occur between the two areas of pattern for the petals. When you pick up the pattern threads, pick up the correct number at the right, then pass the pick-up stick over the number specified for the background and pick up the correct number for the pattern at the left. When picking up the background threads, pick up the correct number at the right-hand selvedge, pass over the number specified for the pattern, pick up the correct number for the background between the petals, pass over the number specified for the second petal, and pick up the correct number for the background at the left-hand selvedge. After you finish row 55, weave 1 in (2.5 cm) in two separate layers, using the same treadling sequence employed for the 1 in (2.5 cm) at the beginning. This completes the exercises in the book. Three projects remain.

# PROJECT 5:
# How to Weave a Crossed-Warp Hanging

The directions for doing the crossed-warp hanging are offered through the kindness of Libby Crawford of Michigan, who uses them regularly for one of the projects in her double-weave workshops. The crossed-warp hanging is made with a series of strips woven in double-width fabric, with areas of open warp threads between the strips. When the second strip is woven, the layers are reversed, thereby causing the warp threads to cross. The side left open in the double-width fabric may also be reversed. In weaving the third strip, the layers are again reversed, again causing the warp threads to cross. The areas left open between the woven strips are from two and a half to three times as long as the warp is wide.

## Preparing the Warp

To make a finished hanging approximately 8 in (20 cm) wide by 36 in (81 cm) long plus fringe, prepare a warp 3½ yd (3.2 m) in length. The choice of yarn depends on the effect you wish to create. Libby Crawford likes to use two related colors, such as blue and green, in a silky yarn; she then threads the outer two thirds of the warp on each layer, with color A on harnesses 1 and 3 and color B on harnesses 2 and 4. The middle third has color A on harnesses 2 and 4, with color B on harnesses 1 and 3, on each layer. A similar arrangement, using a textured or shiny yarn for the weft colors with a smooth warp yarn, would also prove effective. The directions given for this project are for using two contrasting colors of No. 5 perle cotton at 16 ends per inch (2.5 cm) for each layer, with color A on harnesses 1 and 3 and color B on harnesses 2 and 4. Color A weft is used for the first and third woven strips, with harnesses 1 and 3 as the top layer; color B weft is used for the middle strip, with harnesses 2 and 4 as the top layer.

*Figuring the Warp Yarn Needed.* A warp 8 in (20 cm) wide of color A on harnesses 1 and 3 at 16 ends per inch = 128 ends of color A (8 × 16) × 3½ yd (3.2 m) of warp length = 448 yd (408 m) of color A needed for the warp.

A warp 8 in (20 cm) wide of color B on harnesses 2 and 4 at 16 ends per inch = 128 ends of color B (8 × 16) × 3½ yd (3.2 m) of warp length = 448 yd (408 m) of color B needed for the warp.

*Figuring the Weft Yarn Needed.* Two strips woven in weft color A at 2 in (5 cm) for each strip = 4 in (10 cm) woven in weft color A. Allow about 10 in (25 cm) of weft yarn for each shot for each layer (8 in or 20 cm plus take-up) to make 20 in (50 cm) of weft yarn needed for each weft shot × 16 weft shots per inch (2.5 cm) of weaving = 320 in (813 cm) (20 × 16) or approximately 10 yd (9 m) of weft yarn needed for each inch (2.5 cm). 4 in (10 cm) × 10 yd (9 m) = 40 yd (36 m) of color A weft yarn needed. One strip woven in weft color B at 2 in (5 cm) × 10 yd (9 m) of weft yarn per inch (2.5 cm) = 20 yd (18 m) of color B weft yarn needed.

Total color A yarn needed: 448 yd (408 m) for warp + 40 yd (36 m) for weft = 488 yd (444 m)

Total color B yarn needed: 448 yd (408 m) for warp + 20 yd (18 m) for weft = 468 yd (426 m)

No. 5 perle cotton has about 132 yd (120 m) per ounce; approximately four ounces of yarn is needed of each of the two colors to do Project 5.

*Threading the Loom.* Use a straight threading with color A on harnesses 1 and 3 and color B on harnesses 2 and 4. The warp should be sleyed four per dent (two ends of color A and two ends of color B) in an eight-dent reed.

## TO WEAVE THE CROSSED-WARP HANGING

Before starting the weaving, leave 12 in (30 cm) of warp unwoven to use for hanging the piece.

*Step 1.* To weave the first strip with color A weft and harnesses 1 and 3 as the top layer, leaving the right-hand side open, start with the color A weft shuttle at the left-hand selvedge. Weave 2 in (5 cm) as follows:

Raise harness 1. Weave one shot from left to right on the top layer.
Raise harness 3. Weave one shot from right to left on the top layer.
Raise harnesses 1 and 3 plus 4. Weave one shot from left to right on the bottom layer.
Raise harnesses 1 and 3 plus 2. Weave one shot from right to left on the bottom layer.

Harness 2 is raised for the last shot on the bottom layer. When the layers are reversed, to bring harnesses 2 and 4 as the top layer, harness 2 will be used for the first shot to make a smoother exchange of layers. With the color A weft for the first woven strip, the top layer will have a solid color A warp and weft, but the bottom layer will have a color A weft with a color B warp.

If you want to add stiffness to the woven strips, small bamboo sticks can be put in with the weft yarn in the last shot of the top layer and the first shot of the bottom layer when weaving the last sequence before leaving the open warp areas between strips. If you want to manipulate the hanging to make it cylindrical, you can insert flexible wire or colorful chenille pipe cleaners along with the weft in those two shots. The bamboo sticks or wire should be held in place with a series of half hitches made with the weft yarn every three or four threads across the width of the warp. After you have inserted the wire or sticks, be sure to weave the last shot for the bottom layer. Cut off the color A weft yarn, leaving about 3 in (8 cm) to be woven down the selvedge with a needle when the piece comes off the loom.

*Step 2.* Leave an area of open warp two and a half to three times as long as the width of the warp. The warp width for this project is 8 in (20 cm); leave a space of unwoven warp threads 20 to 22 in (50 to 55 cm) long.

*Step 3.* To weave the second strip, with color B weft and harnesses 2 and 4 as the top layer, with the left-hand side open, start with the color B weft shuttle at the right-hand selvedge. Weave 2 in (5 cm) as follows:

Raise harness 2. Weave one shot from right to left on the top layer.
Raise harness 4. Weave one shot from left to right on the top layer.
Raise harnesses 2 and 4 plus 3. Weave one shot from right to left on the bottom layer.
Raise harnesses 2 and 4 plus 1. Weave one shot from left to right on the bottom layer.

Harness 1 is raised for the last shot on the bottom layer; when the layers are reversed to bring harnesses 1 and 3 as the top layer for the third strip, harness 1 will be used for the first shot to make a smoother exchange of layers. With a color B weft for the second strip, the top layer will be a solid color B warp and weft, but the bottom layer will have a color B weft with a color A warp. Again, stiff or flexible material can be inserted with the weft at the bottom and at the top of this strip during the weaving process.

Cut off the color B weft, leaving about 3 in (8 cm) to be woven with a needle down the selvedge when the piece comes off the loom.

*Step 4.* Weave the third strip with color A weft and leave the right-hand side open. Weave 2 in (5 cm) using the sequence of Step 1, with harnesses 1 and 3 as the top layer and harnesses 2 and 4 as the bottom layer. Add the sticks or the wire at the beginning and at the end of this strip, if you wish. Cut off the color A weft, leaving about 3 in (8 cm) to be woven down the selvedge.

*Step 5.* Leave about 12 in (31 cm) of unwoven warp at the top to be used for fringe or braids at the bottom.

*Suggestions:* Beads or small bells may be placed on the wire or sticks to add interest to the hanging. For example, beads could be threaded onto the wire; as the wire is put in place during the weaving, the beads could be spaced at intervals across the width of the warp.

After the piece is taken off the loom, weave the weft ends down along the selvedges. The warp ends left unwoven at the top may be knotted together to use for hanging your weaving. If you used wire or the chenille pipe cleaners in the strips, you can form a cylindrical hanging by manipulating the wire. When cylindrical weavings hang free to move with the movement of air, small bells added to the fringe can be very pleasing.

For a change of pace on a flat wall hanging, try using simple braids at the bottom instead of fringe. The four-strand braid works very well with the two colors in the warp.

# How to Weave a Three-Dimensional Warp-Faced Sampler

Project 6 is designed to show some of the possible applications of double weave in producing sculptural or three-dimensional weavings. Tubes, woven and then stuffed on or off the loom, can be formed into interesting shapes; the projects by Ruth Geneslaw pictured in this book are fine examples of this art. Project 6 demonstrates other possibilities, such as inserting sticks or flexible tubes into lengthwise-woven strips to allow for manipulation off the loom. Weaving flaps on one layer against the smooth background on the other layer will be achieved even without a double beam on the loom. Additional wefts are laid in-between layers, to be used later for braiding or fingerweaving in order to add surface interest to the piece.

The yarn chosen for the sampler is a polished 8/5 linen; a stiff fabric with a shiny surface will be produced because of the density of the warp. In a warp-faced piece, the weft goes through the fabric with very little interaction with the warp. There is a great amount of take-up in the warp, almost double the length of the woven area.

To determine how many ends are needed per inch (2.5 cm), wrap the yarn around a piece of cardboard until the surface is completely covered; count the number of threads in one inch (2.5 cm), and double this amount for the number of ends to the inch (2.5 cm) in making the warp. The warp sett for Project 6 is 24 ends of 8/5 linen to the inch (2.5 cm). Part of the sampler is woven as single-layer fabric and part is double-layered.

## MAKING THE WARP

The warp is 4 in (10 cm) wide and 3½ yd (3.2 m) long. The warp sett of 24 ends to the inch (2.5 cm) is for the single-layer fabric; when double-weave techniques are used, each layer has 12 ends to the inch (2.5 cm).

### Figuring the Warp Yarn Needed

The warp is 4 in (10 cm) wide × 24 ends to the inch (2.5 cm) = 96 warp ends × 3½ yd (3.2 m) long = 336 yd (306 m) of warp yarn needed.

### Figuring the Weft for a 30-in (76-cm)-Long Sampler

There won't be as much take-up in the weft as there is in the warp. Allowing 4½ in (11.3 cm) of weft yarn would be ample for a single shot of weft; however, double wefting will be used and 9 in (23 cm) of yarn should be allowed for each weft shot. The overall number of weft shots per inch (2.5 cm) will average eight. 8 shots × 9 in (23 cm) per shot = 72 in (183 cm) or 2 yd (1.8 m) of weft yarn per inch (2.5 cm) × 30 in (76 cm) = 60 yd of weft yarn needed for the weaving. Add another 30 yd (27 m) for the additional wefts to be laid in for fingerweaving or braiding for a total of 90 yd (82 m) of weft yarn needed for the project. Adding the warp yardage (336 yd or 306 m) to the weft yardage (90 yd or 82 m) makes a total of 426 yd (388 m) of 8/5 linen needed for the project.

Two separate warps will be made; one to be beamed on the loom and the other to be suspended at the back of the loom if you don't have a second beam. Each warp will have 12 warp ends to the inch (2.5 cm) × 4 or 48 warp threads, each 3½ yd (3.2 m) long. One warp will be threaded on harnesses 1 and 3 and the other on harnesses 2 and 4 for a straight threading, 1–2–3–4.

*Threading the Loom.* Beam warp 1 on the loom. If you're accustomed to threading before beaming, the warp should be threaded on harnesses 1 and 3 with one heddle on harness 2 placed between the threads on harnesses 1 and 3 and one heddle on harness 4 placed between the threads on harnesses 3 and 1. In other words, thread the first end of the warp on the first heddle on harness 1; next place an unthreaded heddle on harness 2 in position; and then thread the second end through the first heddle on harness 3. Before threading the third end on harness 1, place an unthreaded heddle on harness 4 in position. Continue threading the warp in this manner until all 48 ends are threaded.

After warp 1 is beamed on, thread the ends of warp 2 on harnesses 2 and 4 through the heddles placed in position between the ends of warp 1. If you have a second beam on your loom, beam warp 2 onto the second warp beam.

## How to Suspend Warp 2 at the Back of the Loom

Secure the ends of warps 1 and 2 to the cloth beam at the front of the loom; next unchain warp 2 at the back of the loom. Using six ends of the warp, make a loop at a point 15 in (38.1 cm) below the back beam. Make a loop with every six ends across the warp, taking care to have the loops all at the same level. Warp 2 is kept separate from warp 1 because the threads on harnesses 2 and 4 will be used to weave elongated flaps.

There are numerous ways to achieve tension on suspended warp ends:

1. You can place a smooth metal rod or thick dowel through the loops and hang weights on the rod or dowel. The weights can be pieces of metal, or bricks tied on with cords placed through the holes in the bricks. My favorite way is to tie empty bottles onto each end of the rod; if extra tension is needed, water can be poured into the bottles to add extra weight. (Bottles with handles and screw-on tops are especially good.)
2. You can place rocks or other objects in small cloth bags, which are then tied to the loops on the warp ends. Old nylon stockings or pantyhose work very well to hold the weights.
3. The rod itself can be a heavy lead pipe with enough weight to do the job.
4. If you have an extra loom, you can back it against your first loom and then beam warp 2 onto the second loom.

Whatever method you use, the tension on warp 2 should be the same as the tension on warp 1. Whenever the warp is ready to be moved forward, check to see that the warp ends are suspended properly. If necessary, take the rod and the weights off and retie the loops farther down on the warp ends.

## TO WEAVE THE WARP-FACED SAMPLER

### Section 1: Plain Weave with Double Wefting

Cut a length of 8/5 linen at least 3 yd (2.7 m) long. Make a butterfly at each end or wind each end onto a separate small, flat shuttle, leaving the center 18 in (46 cm) free.

Raise harnesses 1 and 3. Place the weft yarn through the shed with the center of the yarn at the midpoint of the width of the warp and with one shuttle or butterfly of yarn on each selvedge. Beat firmly.

Raise harnesses 2 and 4. With a sword or a shuttle, beat inside the shed to make the exchange of threads as firm as possible. Next pass the weft yarn at the right-hand selvedge through the shed from right to left; in the same shed, pass the weft yarn at the left-hand selvedge through from left to right. This is known as double wefting. Beat firmly. The weft yarn can be seen at each selvedge but should not be visible between the warp threads.

Weave 3 in (8 cm) in plain weave, alternately raising harnesses 1 and 3 for one shot and harnesses 2 and 4 for the other shot, each time beating inside the shed with a sword or shuttle before passing the double weft through the shed.

### Section 2: Weave Three Separate Strips With Sticks or Tubes in the Double-Weave Areas

This area will be woven in three strips, with a 2-in (5-cm) strip in the center and a 1-in (2.5-cm) strip on each side. A separate double weft will be used for each strip.

Weave 1 in (2.5 cm) in plain weave, taking care to keep the wefts of each strip separate; if there is any crossing of wefts, the strips cannot be spread apart later when the strips are manipulated.

Weave ½ in (1.3 cm) in two separate layers, keeping the three strips separate from each other. Use a single weft for each layer in the following four-step sequence:

Raise harness 1. Weave one shot with weft A.
Raise harness 3. Weave one shot with weft A.
Raise harnesses 1 and 3 plus 2. Weave one shot with weft B.
Raise harnesses 1 and 3 plus 4. Weave one shot with weft B.

After weaving ½ in (1.3 cm), raise harnesses 1 and 3; place a narrow stick about 8 in (20 cm) long through the opening. Raise harnesses 2 and 4 and begin double wefting in plain weave on the three strips. Weave 3 in (8 cm) in plain weave with the double wefts. Weave a ¼ in (0.7 cm) area in two separate layers, using the sequence just described, with a single weft for each layer of each strip. Raise harnesses 1 and 3 and place an 8-in (20-cm) piece of flexible tubing in the opening. The small plastic tubing used in fish tanks works very well. The tubing is cut when the weaving comes off the loom; the two outside 1-in (2.5-cm) strips are brought together over the top of the center 2-in (5-cm) strip and sewn together by threading yarn through the opening in the tubes. Details will be given later.

Raise harnesses 2 and 4 to begin plain weave with double wefting on the three strips. Weave 3 in (8 cm) in plain weave. Weave an area ½ in (1.3 cm) long in two separate layers with a single weft for each layer of each strip. Raise harnesses 1 and 3 and insert a narrow stick about 8 in (20 cm) long through the opening. Raise harnesses 2 and 4 to begin plain weave with double wefting on the three strips. Weave 3 in (8 cm) in plain weave.

## Section 3: Plain Weave With Double Wefting

In Section 3, the warp will no longer be divided into three strips. Weave 2 in (5.1 cm) in plain weave with double wefting, going all the way across the warp with one pair of double wefts.

## Section 4: Laying In Extra Wefts for Fingerweaving or Braiding

Section 4 is a series of areas of two-layered fabric, with extra wefts laid in as the layers are exchanged. Before starting the weaving, cut 12 lengths of weft yarn, each one 2½ yd (2.3 m) long.

Weave ¼ in (7 mm) in two separate layers, with harnesses 1 and 3 as the top layer and harnesses 2 and 4 as the bottom layer. Raise harnesses 1 and 3; insert four of the extra wefts in the opening, with an equal amount of yarn hanging out at each side.

Weave ¼ in (7 mm) in two separate layers, this time with harnesses 2 and 4 as the top layer and harnesses 1 and 3 as the bottom layer. Raise harnesses 2 and 4; insert four more of the extra wefts in the opening, with an equal amount of yarn hanging out at each side. Weave ¼ in (7 mm) in two separate layers, with harnesses 1 and 3 returning as the top layer and harnesses 2 and 4 as the bottom layer. Raise harnesses 1 and 3; lay in the last 4 extra wefts as you did before.

## Section 5: Plain Weave and Open Warp Areas

Raise harnesses 2 and 4 to start plain weave with double wefting. Use a single pair of wefts all across the warp. Continue in plain weave for 2 in (5.1 cm).

Leave an area of warp unwoven for about 2 in (5.1 cm). Weave another 2 in (5.1 cm) in plain weave with double wefting.

## Section 6: Weaving Flaps on One Layer Against a Background on the Other Layer

In Section 6, harnesses 2 and 4 are woven as the top layer and harnesses 1 and 3 are woven as the bottom layer. Two separate layers are woven, but the top layer is woven longer than the bottom layer and then fastened in place against the bottom layer. The result is a raised flap of the top layer of fabric, for a sculptural effect.

Start by weaving 1 in (2.5 cm) in two separate layers, remembering to use harnesses 2 and 4 for the top layer. The density of the warp is 12 ends to the inch;

you can produce a thicker fabric by using a double weft or by using a heavier yarn for the weft for each layer. Weave only the top layer on harnesses 2 and 4 for 2 in (5.1 cm) more, leaving the bottom layer unwoven.

Raise harnesses 1 and 3 to start weaving in plain weave, pulling the fabric woven on harnesses 2 and 4 back until the end of this flap is even with the end of the 1 in (2.5 cm) woven on harnesses 1 and 3. Use double wefting for the plain weave. If you have difficulty holding the flap in place initially, insert a dowel into the first plain weave shed; secure the ends of the dowel to the front beam with strong cord. Weave the first and second shots of the plain weave; remove the dowel and use a sword to beat the inside of the shed to close the gap created by the dowel. Weave 1 in (2.5 cm) in plain weave.

Repeat the process for weaving flaps, starting again at the beginning with the 1 in (2.5 cm) in two separate layers, with harnesses 2 and 4 as the top layer and harnesses 1 and 3 as the bottom layer. If you feel more adventuresome, try weaving two separate flaps on the top layer or even three. This time, weave the top layer for 4 in (10 cm) instead of 2 in (5.1 cm); when the fabric of the top layer is brought back to be made even with the bottom layer, the flap created will be even greater than the first one. If you wish, lay thin wire in with the weft in one or two places when weaving the top layer; later this wire can be used to shape the woven flap.

### Section 7: Plain Weave With Double Wefting

End the sampler by weaving 2 in (5.1 cm) of plain weave.

### Finishing the Sampler

After the sampler comes off the loom, work with the section of three separate strips. Spread the three strips apart on the narrow stick. Cut the thin flexible tube into three sections, leaving enough on each side of each strip to assure that the weaving does not come off. Using a length of the weft yarn, thread the yarn through the tube of the right-hand, 1-in (2.5-cm) strip, and then through the tube of the left-hand, 1-in (2.5-cm) strip. Pull the tubes out of the openings, leaving the yarn in place. Position the two 1-in (2.5-cm) strips above the center 2-in (5.1-cm) strip; thread one end of the yarn through the tube of the center strip and pull the tube out of the opening, leaving the yarn in place. Using a needle or crochet hook, pull the other end of the yarn through the same space on the center strip. Pull the ends of the yarn until the two 1-in (2.5-cm) strips are firmly in place above the center strip. Using a needle, thread one end of the yarn back through the weaving for three or four rows in one direction, and the other end back through the weaving for three or four rows in the other direction. Cut off the extra yarn.

To finish the extra wefts added in Section 4, make braids or narrow fingerwoven strips on each side. Bring the strips to the front of the woven piece and pass them through the center of the unwoven area of Section 5 to the back of the fabric. Next bring the strips around to the center front above the lower 2-in (5-cm) plain weave section of Section 5. Using a needle, thread the ends through to the back, two ends at a time, one from each strip. Secure the ends at the back by threading a few at a time through the rows of weaving to lie parallel with the weft threads. Cut off the excess yarn. The sampler is now finished, and should furnish ideas for weaving larger sculptural projects.

## PROJECT 7:
# How to Weave a Table Runner With a Holiday Motif Using the Pick-Up Design Technique

Project 7 is based on a table runner designed and woven by Laurene Ouellette, a Fine Arts graduate from the College of New Rochelle. The yarn used for the runner is a 16/2 linen at 20 ends per inch (2.5 cm) for each layer, with white for one layer on harnesses 1 and 3 and red for the other layer on harnesses 2 and 4.

The finished dimensions of the runner are 24 in (61 cm) wide by 72 in (183 cm) long plus an allowance of 5 in (13 cm) at each end for fringe. The design which is 20 in (51 cm) wide by 44 in (112 cm) long is placed in the center area. The table for which the runner was designed is 30 in (76 cm) wide by 48 in (122 cm) long, thereby permitting the holiday pattern to be seen in its entirety when the runner is placed on the table.

The design, with holly leaves and arrangements of candles, was first drawn to scale to show the overall pattern (see Figure 38). Next the first area of the pattern, the holly leaves and berries above the border, was transferred to graph paper in order to square up the design (see Figure 39). Each small square on the graph represents two warp threads in width and two weft rows in height. The first row of the holly pattern starts three squares above the top row of the border; the area of design to be picked up for that row is one square wide and one square high, which means that two warp threads would be picked up for the pattern and two weft rows would be woven.

The area that is drawn in to the right of the holly leaves is the beginning of the first candle in the grouping on the right-hand side of the design. The grouping of the three large candles and flames was transferred to graph paper, maintaining the same scale of two warp threads and two weft rows represented by each square (see Figure 40). The design is shown as it appears on the right half of the runner; if you refer to the overall design, you'll see that an identical grouping occurs on the left-hand side of the holly leaves in a balanced arrangement, with the first candle of the group being the one closest to the center of the runner. The diagram for the first candle is 15 squares in width, which represents 30 warp threads to be picked up; the diagram for the first candle is 52 squares high, which represents 104 weft rows. The candles are 5 squares apart, which represents 10 background warp threads. At the left-hand side of the candle diagram, the edge of the right-hand holly leaf is drawn in to show the relationship of the two design areas.

Figure 38. *Holiday motif for a table runner.*

The pattern for the center of the runner is balanced both in length and in width; the design transferred to graph paper shows the right-hand half, beginning with the border at the edge, leading up to the larger candle at the center, and going through the smaller candle on the other side of the center of the table runner (see Figure 41). The left-hand side of the design is the opposite of the right-hand side, but the dimensions of the individual design elements are identical. By counting the number of squares in width and multiplying by two, you can determine how many pattern or background threads to pick up for a given row of the design; by counting the number of squares in height and multiplying by two, you can determine how many weft rows should be woven, once the warp has been made and threaded on the loom.

## MAKING THE WARP

For a finished runner 24 in (61 cm) wide by 72 in (183 cm) long plus fringe, a warp 25 in (63.5 cm) wide by 3½ yd (3.2 m) long is planned. The extra inch (2.5 cm) in

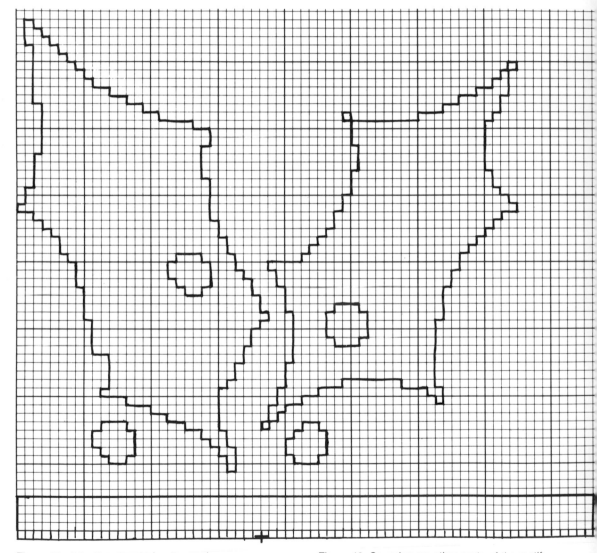

**Figure 39.** *Adapting the design to graph paper.*          **Figure 40.** *Squaring up other parts of the motif.*

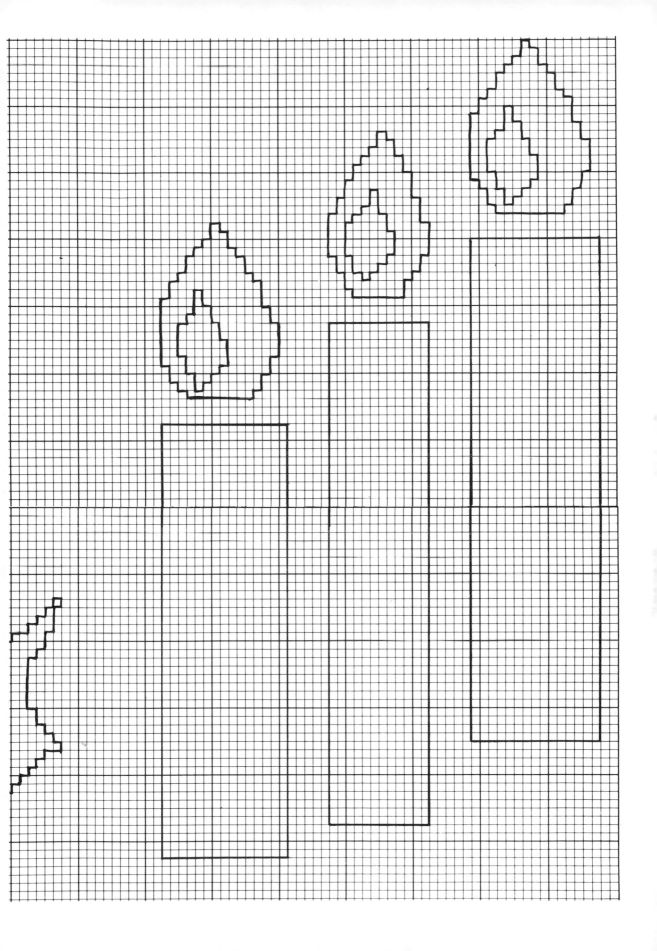

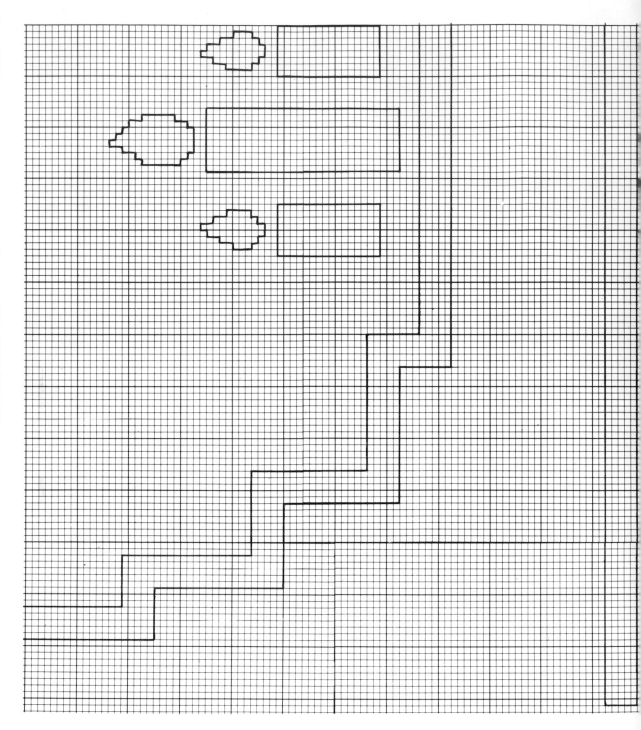

Figure 41. *Finishing the design transfer.*

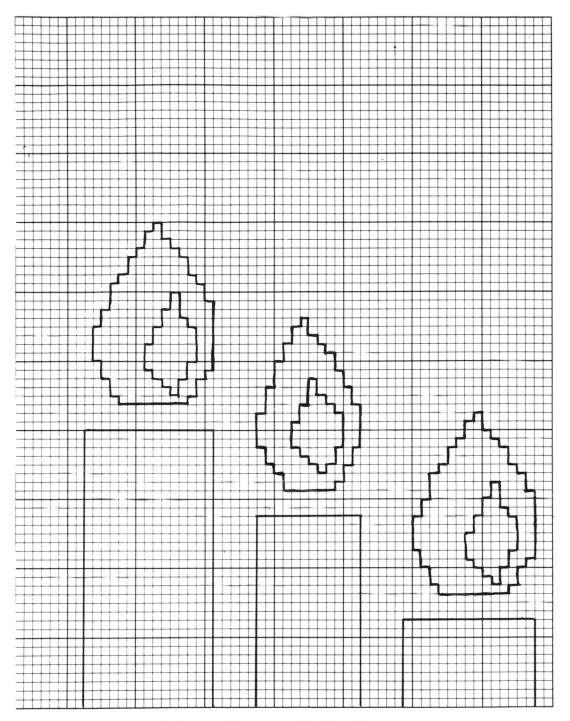

**Figure 42.** *Reversing the candle design for the opposite side of the table runner.*

width allows for approximately five percent take-up in the width, and the 3½-yd (3.2-m) length allows for 1 yd (0.9 m) of loom waste, plus the lengthwise take-up.

The yardage needed for the warp is as follows:

Color A (white) 20 ends per inch (2.5 cm) × 25 in (63.5 cm) wide = 500 ends × 3½ yd (3.2 m) long = 1750 yd (1593 m) of color A warp yarn needed
Color B (red) 20 ends per inch (2.5 cm) × 25 in (63.5 cm) wide = 500 ends × 3½ yd (3.2 m) long = 1750 yd (1593 m) of color B warp yarn needed

A balanced or 50/50 weave with as many weft shots to the inch (2.5 cm) as there are warp ends to the inch (2.5 cm) would require approximately as much weft yarn as warp yarn yardage. 3500 yd (3186 m) of color A and 3500 yd (3186 m) of color B should be a sufficient amount of yarn for the project.

*Threading the Loom.* Use a straight threading, 1–2–3–4, with color A (white) on harnesses 1 and 3 and color B (red) on harnesses 2 and 4.

*Sleying the Reed.* Use a 10-dent reed with four ends per dent (two of color A and two of color B) or a 20-dent reed with two ends per dent, one of each color. In the first two dents at each end, the threads could be doubled to give a better selvedge.

## TO WEAVE THE TABLE RUNNER

Color A (white) on harnesses 1 and 3 is the background color for the top layer; color B (red) on harnesses 2 and 4 is the pattern color for the top layer.

Before starting the weaving, leave 5 in (13 cm) of warp unwoven to use as fringe. The design area of the runner is the center 44 in (112 cm) in length leaving 28 in (122 cm) left from the overall 72-in (183-cm) length; there will be 14 in (36 cm) at the beginning and 14 in (36 cm) at the end, woven without any pick-up work (14 + 44 + 14 = 72).

*Step 1.* Weave 14 in (36 cm) in two separate layers, with color A on harnesses 1 and 3 as the top layer and color B on harnesses 2 and 4 as the bottom layer, using the following four-step sequence:

Raise harness 1. Weave one shot of color A weft.
Raise harness 3. Weave one shot of color A weft.
Raise harnesses 1 and 3 plus 2. Weave one shot of color B weft.
Raise harnesses 1 and 3 plus 4. Weave one shot of color B weft.

*Step 2.* To weave the border pattern below the holly leaves: The border design is 40 squares wide on each side of the center, for a total width of 80 squares, representing 160 pattern color B warp ends to be picked up. The border is 5 squares high or 10 weft rows in height. The eight-step pick-up sequence weaves two rows for each layer; five repeats of the sequence would produce the 10 rows needed to weave a color B border on a color A background on the top layer. The same pattern will appear on the bottom layer, with the colors reversed.

On either side of the 160 pattern warp ends, there will be 170 background warp ends. To make it easier to pick up the correct threads, use a thin thread of a different color to lay in the shed under the center four warp ends.

The eight-step pick-up sequence to be used for all the areas of pattern for the table runner is as follows:

Raise harnesses 2 and 4. Using a pick-up stick, pick up the pattern threads from the color B warp ends. Lower harnesses 2 and 4.
Raise harness 1. Clear the shed. Pass the color A weft through the shed. Remove the pick-up stick and beat.
Raise harnesses 1 and 3. Pick up the background warp threads from the color A warp ends. Lower harnesses 1 and 3.
Raise harness 2. Clear the shed. Pass the color B weft through the shed. Remove the pick-up stick and beat.
Raise harnesses 2 and 4. Pick up the same pattern threads from the color B warp ends. Lower harnesses 2 and 4.
Raise harness 3. Clear the shed. Pass the color A weft through the shed. Remove the pick-up stick and beat.
Raise harnesses 1 and 3. Pick up the same background threads from the color A warp ends. Lower harnesses 1 and 3.
Raise harness 4. Clear the shed. Pass the color B weft through the shed. Remove the pick-up stick and beat.

The pattern threads to be picked up for the border design in this area are the center 160 color B threads; in picking up the background threads, pick up 170 color A warp ends, pass over the center 160 ends, and pick up the other 170 color A warp ends left. Weaving through the entire eight-step sequence five times will complete this area.

*Step 3.* To weave the three squares between the top of the border design and the beginning of the holly-leaves pattern, use the same four-step sequence employed in Step 1 to weave the beginning 14 in (36 cm). Three repeats of that sequence will produce the six rows of each layer represented by the three squares in height.

*Step 4.* To weave the holly and candle design area, the holly leaves and berries will be started first. Count the squares out from the center as they are shown on the diagram until you reach an area outlined for the pattern. Each square not outlined for the design represents two background warp threads to be picked up in color A; each square outlined for the design represents two pattern warp threads to be picked up in color B. For each row in height, one repeat of the eight-step sequence of Step 2 must be woven. Notice that in each holly leaf there is an area where the background color A warps will be picked up.

At a point 21 squares above the top of the border design, the first row of the centermost candles occurs. The width of the candles is 15 squares or 30 threads each; there are 21 squares between the candle design and the holly design at that point, representing 42 color A background warp ends. To pick up the pattern for this row, pick up the correct color B warp ends for the holly leaves, pass the pick-up stick over 42 warp ends to the right and 42 to the left, and then pick up 30 color B warp ends for the candle to the right of the center and 30 color B warp ends for the candle to the left of the center.

If you weave this area row by row, counting the squares and noting whether the design area becomes larger or smaller, you'd be adding or dropping only a few pattern or background threads as the design changes.

*Note:* Be sure to reverse the design of the flames for the left-hand candles so that they slant from the center upward as they appear on the overall design (see Figure 42).

*Step 5.* To weave the area from the top of the flames to the beginning of the center design, weave 1½ in (3.8 cm)—30 rows on each layer—using the four-step sequence of Step 1.

*Step 6.* To weave the center design area: If you refer to Figure 41, you'll see that the first part of the design in this area is the border pattern stripe, 5 squares or 10 warp threads in width. This border stripe starts at a point 2½ in (6.3 cm) in from the selvedge on each side; when picking up this pattern area, pass the stick over 50 warp threads at each selvedge, pick up 10 warp ends at each side for the stripes, passing over all the other center warp threads. After weaving the stripes for 10 squares in height, or 10 repeats of the eight-step pick-up sequence, the beginning of the inner design occurs.

The diagram represents the right-hand side of the design; the reverse of the design is picked up for the left-hand side. There are 25 squares shown for the right-hand side; therefore 50 squares or 100 color B warp threads should be picked up for the bottom part of the inner design area. To pick up the first row, pass over the first 50 threads, pick up 10 ends for the right-hand stripe, pass over 140 threads, pick up the center 100 ends; then pass over 140 threads, pick up 10 ends for the left-hand stripe, and pass over the last 50 threads.

Weave the center design area row by row, referring to the diagram to determine which pattern and which background ends to pick up. The midpoint in the length of the runner is reached when the highest part of the center candle is woven. Reverse the design to weave the second half.

*Step 7.* To weave the area from the end of the center design to the top of the flames for the large candles, weave 1½ in (3.8 cm)—30 rows on each layer—using the four-step sequence of Step 1.

*Step 8.* To weave the second holly and candle design area, reverse the design of Step 4, picking up the flames and candles first and then the holly leaves and berries.

*Step 9.* Weave six rows on each layer using the four-step procedure of Step 1.

*Step 10.* To weave the border pattern above the holly leaves, repeat Step 2, picking up the center color B warp ends for the pattern and weaving 10 rows on each layer.

*Step 11.* Weave 14 in (36 cm) in two separate layers, using the four-step sequence as in Step 1, with color A on harnesses 1 and 3 as the top layer and color B on harnesses 2 and 4 as the bottom layer.

The weaving of the runner is now complete; before cutting the warp off the loom, be sure to leave 5 in (13 cm) for the fringe at this end.

# Suppliers List

The Book Barn, Avon Park North, P.O. Box 256, Avon, CT. 06001. *Books.*

Contessa Yarns, P.O. Box 37, Lebanon, CT. 06249. *Wool, cotton, and linen.*

Frederick J. Fawcett, Inc., 129 South Street, Boston, MA. 02111. *Linen and cotton.*

The Mannings, R.D. 2, East Berlin, PA. 17316. *Wool yarn, including CUM and Maypole, Fawcett linen, Lily cotton, and other yarns; books.*

Museum Books, 48 East 43rd Street, New York, N.Y. 10017. *Books.*

School Products Co., 1201 Broadway, New York, N.Y. 10001. *Wool, including CUM yarns, cotton, and linen; books.*

The Silver Shuttle, 1301 35th Street, N.W., Washington, D.C. 20007. *Wool, linen, perle cotton; books.*

Straw Into Gold, P.O. Box 2904S, Oakland, CA. 94618. *Wool, cotton, and linen; books.*

Ulltex, P.O. Box 918, 59 Demond Avenue, North Adams, MA. 01247. *Swedish yarns, including wool, cotton, linen, and cottolin.*

A Weaver and a Potter, 33 Main Street, Newton, CT. 06470. *Wool, including Ulltex Swedish yarns, cotton, and linen; books.*

## GREAT BRITAIN

Campden Weavers, 16 Lower High Street, Chipping Campden, Gloucestershire. *Handweaving yarns.*

Craftsman's Mark Ltd., Trefnant, Denbigh LL16 5UD, North Wales. *Wool, linen, cotton.*

William Hall & Co. (Monsall) Ltd, 177 Stanley Road, Cheadle Hulme, Cheadle, Cheshire SK8 6RF. *Cotton, wool, linen.*

Handweavers Studio & Gallery Ltd., 29 Haroldstone Road, London E17 7AN. *Yarns. Samples and catalog £1.*

The Pantiles Bookshop, 48 The Pantiles, Tunbridge Wells, Kent TN2 5TN. *Books.*

Texere Yarns, 9 Peckover Street, Bradford BD1 5BD, West Yorkshire. *Wool, linen, cotton.*

# Bibliography

*Ancient Peruvian Textiles from the Collection of the Textile Museum, Washington, D.C. and the Museum of Primitive Art, New York.* Introduction and Notes by Mary Elizabeth King. New York: The Museum of Primitive Art, 1965.

Atwater, Mary Meigs. *The Shuttlecraft Book of American Handweaving.* Rev. ed. New York: The Macmillan Company, 1961.

Birrell, Verla. *The Textile Arts.* New York: Harper & Brothers, 1959.

Burnham, Harold B., and Burnham, Dorothy K. *'Keep Me Warm One Night', Early Handweaving in Eastern Canada.* Toronto, Canada: University of Toronto Press, 1972.

Cason, Marjorie, and Cahlander, Adele. *The Art of Bolivian Highland Weaving: Unique, Traditional Techniques for the Modern Weaver.* New York: Watson-Guptill Publications, 1976.

Collingwood, Peter. *The Technique of Rug Making.* New York: Watson-Guptill Publications, 1968.

D'Harcourt, Raoul. *Textiles of Ancient Peru and Their Techniques,* translated by Sadie Brown. Edited by Grace G. Denny and Carolyn M. Osborne. Seattle: University of Washington Press, 1962.

Emery, Irene. *The Primary Structures of Fabrics.* Washington, D.C.: The Textile Museum, 1966.

*Fiber Structures.* Introduction by Irene Emery, published in cooperation with the Handweavers Guild of America, Inc. and the Weavers' Guild of Pittsburgh. New York: Van Nostrand Reinhold Company, 1976.

Oelsner, G. H. *A Handbook of Weaves,* translated and revised by Samuel S. Dale. Original edition by the Macmillan Company in 1915. New York: Dover Publications, 1952.

Tidball, Harriet. *The Double Weave, Plain and Patterned.* Shuttle Craft Monograph One. Lansing, Michigan: The Shuttle Craft Guild, 1960.

Tod, Osma Gallinger. *The Joy of Handweaving.* 2nd ed. New York: Dover Publications, 1977.

Zimmern, Natalie H. *Introduction to Peruvian Costume.* Brooklyn, New York: The Brooklyn Institute of Arts and Sciences: John B. Watkins Company, 1949.

# Index

*Note:* References to photographs or figures are in *italics.*

weft on top, 27; open on left with color B warp and weft on top, 27, 28; open on right with color B warp and weft on top, 26; open on right with solid color A warp and weft on top, 25, 26; pillow, 30–36; saddle bag, 37–39; shoulder bag, 36, 37; stuffed, *81;* two joined at exchange of layers, 24, 25; two or more woven simultaneously, 23, 24; two shuttle, 21
Tubing, flexible, 127–129
Tubular weave, 7, 10, 21–29, 34, *81–83; 89, 92, 96*
Twill, 59, 60; rug, reversible, *85,* 99–102
Two-block design concept, 48, 61
Two separate layers, 29, 41–43; exchanging the, 16, 17; with color A on top, 14, 15; with color B on top, 15, 16

Ulltex, 30, 40, 75
Upholstery, 59

Vest, 49, *89*

Wall hanging, 7; decorations for, *96,* 124; double-weave, layered, *91;* double-weave pick-up, *90, 91, 95;* lace, 18, 19; warp-crossed, *88, 94,* 122–124; warp-faced sculptured, *88*
Warp: color arrangement, *75;* for crossed-warp hanging, 122, 123; for pick-up technique, 104; for pillow, 30, *30,* 31, *31;* for poncho, 40, *40,* 41; for runner, 135; for sampler, 125–127; for throws, 76, 77; for twill rug, 99, 100; open thread,
122; separate, 10–14; sleying the, 28, 31, 41, 100, 104, 123; suspending the, 126–127; threading the, 66, *67,* 99, 100; two-color blanket, 77–80, *79, 84,* 97, 98. *See also* Stripes
Warp, crossed-, hanging, *88, 94,* 122–124; preparing the warp for, 122, 123; weaving the, 123, 124
Warp-faced sampler, *88,* 125–130; finishing the, 129, 130; making the warp for, 125–127; weaving the, 127–129
Warp sett, 30, 40, 125
Warping board (mill), 41
Weave: backstitch, 18; balanced, 51, 135; bog shirt, 40, 43–46, *44, 46, 83;* double, defined, 7, 8; gauze, 20; plaid, 23, 28, 30–33, 36, 37; plain, 8, 10, 28, 29, *81,* 99; plain with double wefting, 127–129; random weft-striped patterned, 43; ruana-style poncho, 40–43; three-dimensional, 78, *96,* 125–130; tubular, 7, 10, 21–29, *81–83, 89, 92, 96*
Weft: double, 127–129; laid-in; *89,* 125, 126, 128; multiple, 7. *See also* Stripes
*Wheat, 92*
Wool, 7, 30, 75, 84, 85, 89, 91–96, 100

Yarn, 10–12, 18, 19, 26, 39, 48, 60, 75, 78, 89, 104, 122, 123, 125, 127–130; for warp yardage, 31, 40, 41, 76, 99, 122, 123, 125, 126, 135; for weft yardage, 14, 41, 78, 80, 97, 98, 100, 122, 123, 125, 126, 136. *See also* Wool

Edited by Bonnie Silverstein
Designed by Bob Fillie
Set in 11-point Helvetica Light